The

Mean Mom's

*Guide to Raising
Great Kids*

The
Mean Mom's
Guide to Raising
Great Kids

Joanne Kraft

LEAFWOOD
P U B L I S H E R S
an imprint of Abilene Christian University Press

THE MEAN MOM'S GUIDE TO RAISING GREAT KIDS

LEAFWOOD
PUBLISHERS
an imprint of Abilene Christian University Press

Copyright © 2015 by Joanne Kraft | ISBN 978-0-89112-442-9 | LCCN 2014045345

Printed in the United States of America

Scripture quotations, unless otherwise noted, are from The Holy Bible, New International Version. Copyright © 2011 by Biblica, Inc.® Used by permission. All rights reserved worldwide.

Scripture quotations marked CEV are from the Contemporary English Version® Copyright © 1995 American Bible Society. All rights reserved.

Scripture quotations noted ESV are from The ESV ® Bible (The Holy Bible, English Standard Version®) copyright © 2001 by Crossway, a publishing ministry of Good News Publishers. ESV ® Text Edition: 2011. All rights reserved.

Scripture quotations noted NLT are taken from the New Living Translation, Copyright © 2007 by Tyndale House Foundation. Used by permission of Tyndale House Publishers, Inc. All rights reserved.

Scriptures noted NKJV are taken from the New King James Version® Copyright © 1982 by Thomas Nelson. Used by permission. All rights reserved.

Scripture quotations noted *The Message* taken from *The Message*. Copyright 2002. Used by permission of NavPress Publishing Group.

Scripture quotations noted KJV are taken from the King James Version of the Bible.

Scripture quotations noted NRSV are taken from the New Revised Standard Version Bible, copyright © 1989, the Division of Christian Education of the National Council of the Churches of Christ in the United States of America. Used by permission. All rights reserved.

Scripture quotations noted NASB taken from the New American Standard Bible, Copyright © 1995 by The Lockman Foundation. Used by permission.

LIBRARY OF CONGRESS CATALOGING-IN-PUBLICATION DATA
Kraft, Joanne.
  The mean mom's guide to raising great kids / Joanne Kraft.
    pages cm
  Includes bibliographical references and index.
  ISBN 978-0-89112-442-9 (alk. paper)
  1. Mother and child--Religious aspects--Christianity. 2. Child rearing--Religious aspects--Christianity.
3. Parenting--Religious aspects--Christianity. I. Title.
  BV4529.18.K73 2015
  248.8'431--dc23

                                                                                    2014045345

Cover design by Beca Clifton and Morgan Bortz | Interior text design by Sandy Armstrong

For information contact:
Abilene Christian University Press, ACU Box 29138, Abilene, Texas 79699

1-877-816-4455 | www.leafwoodpublishers.com

15 16 17 18 19 20 / 7 6 5 4 3 2 1

Grandma Cusumano
Aka: Granny Goose, Gramma Cuckoo, Cuckoo Bird
How did I get the best Grandma in the whole wide world?
Makes me sad for everyone else.
I love you,
Joey
P.S. You were never mean.

Acknowledgments

The idea for *The Mean Mom's Guide to Raising Great Kids* came to light in a police communications center in Folsom, California. (I love you ladies and miss you like crazy). If the world only knew how many parents call the police department in need of a little *mean mom* wisdom.

Much thanks to the best Mean Mom Team around and their unofficial captain, Katie Chaney. When I asked for help, you immediately raised your hands. You're wise beyond your years, and humble enough to share. Many moms will be encouraged by your words woven throughout this book—they bring the sparkle. Your prayers for each reader will give this book wings.

Jennifer Sienes—thank you, friend. You allowed me to throw chapters your way when your life was so busy. Chris Pedersen and Elizabeth Thompson—my Inspire (InspireWriters.com) girls and the best author-writer-editor friends a gal can have. So glad I joined Inspire Christian Writers so many years ago.

Gary Myers—thank you for believing in this project. Mary Hardegree and the Leafwood publishing team—I'm so grateful for your supernatural patience and helping hands. I promise, no more edits.

Angela Mackey, Julie Sanders, Marci Seither, Jessica Wolstenholm, Tara Dovenbarger, and Melissa Mashburn—you selflessly shared your words, and I'm so grateful.

Celia—thank you for believing in me from the very beginning.

Meghan, David, Grace, and Samuel—you four are the biggest pieces of my heart. Thank you for giving me much to write about. I'm proud to be your mom and I think you're great kids. My next book's dedication page is up for grabs. No pressure.

Paul—my husband and best friend, how do I thank you for so much? Your hard work allows me to stay home with the kids, garden, bake, clean the house (sometimes), and write. I love you so. Let's grab a coffee and take a long country drive.

To my Lord and Savior, Jesus Christ, because of you I live and love. My words fall painfully short. Thank you, Father. I love you.

Contents

Prologue

Does the phrase *mean mom* make you a little nervous? Are memories of an unhappy childhood rushing back? Or are you slightly intrigued? Are you envisioning a few "Mommy Dearest" lessons with wire hangers or torturous time-outs? Oh my! Then you're way off base.

First things first. The *Mean Mom's Guide* is not about discouraging children's hearts, stifling their creativity, or controlling their God-given gifts.

The *Mean Mom's Guide* is written from one mom to another. It's about encouraging a few of us overly sweet *marshmallow moms* to instill much-needed boundaries in the lives of our children. It's about enabling confidence in your God-given inner voice and learning to be okay on those occasions when your kids don't like you.

Mean moms look like any other mom. They don't conform to nice parenting because their friends are doing it. They don't live for the moment but use every moment for the bigger picture—to raise children who will become emotionally strong, responsible, independent, and productive God-honoring adults.

Every child is different, which means parenting styles are different, too. This book was written with the help of more than one hundred and fifty women who have walked in your shoes. Their words of wisdom and encouragement will inspire you to stick with it even when it's hard. While reading each chapter, you need to remember one thing: the word *mean* isn't always the "mean" you think it means.

Go and pour yourself a cup of tea, or bring your nonfat vanilla latte to the couch, and kick off your shoes. Let's have ourselves a little chat about our kids.

PART ONE

The Making of a Mean Mom

CHAPTER ONE

Are You a Mean Mom?

- -

I'm always entertained by the use of the word "mean." Kids who use it are often the ones least likely to have any idea what "mean" truly means.
—Michelle McDonald, sportswriter for ESPN

*C*all me crazy, but moms are becoming nicer. There used to be a time when kids could spend hours regaling one another with mean mom stories. I know it used to be a favorite pastime of mine.

"My mom is the meanest. Listen to this. . . ." I brush aside my big '80s feathered hair for emphasis. "She wouldn't let me come over today until *after* my homework was finished and *after* I cleaned the kitchen," I complained to my girlfriend.

"If you think your mom is mean, Joanne, listen to this one. . . ."

Legendary stories have gathered over time—too many to recount. My parenting style has been molded and shaped by them. As far as I was concerned, my mom was the meanest of all. She wanted to know who my friends were and what I was watching on

TV. She upheld curfews, expected me to do well in school, and paid close attention to what I wore.

Mean Mom Flashback

I was hoping to slip out the front door before my parents caught a glimpse of my outfit. I was a typical sixteen-year-old, and I just knew they wouldn't be able to hear the whisper of "cool" announcing my presence. Nor would they understand that my black stretch pants made a statement.

Unfortunately, I had never learned the art of Navy Seal stealth operations, and my mom intercepted my exit. "Sweetheart, what are you wearing?"

Questions asking the obvious are the bane of every teenager's existence. "Black pants," I blurted, searching for an escape route.

"Those are not black pants. Those are skintight." She called for backup. "George!"

Dad is a former U.S. Marine, so I knew he would be up for a battle. I would lose this skirmish. Mom would make sure of it.

"What in the world are those?" He looked down at my legs, his face scrunched up as if he were in the presence of something extraterrestrial.

My earlier confidence squeaked out as a pathetic question hoping for approval. "Black pants?"

With Dad as her wingman, my one-and-only "mean mom" began her rant: "No daughter of mine. . . ."

Yep, here we go. The "no daughter of mine" speech.

As you can imagine, my response was predictable. I was angry with my mean mom. I stomped off to my room and whimpered over my shoulder, "Mom. You are so *mean!*" Needless to say, I never left the house in those skintight stretch pants.

Fast-forward thirty years. Yesterday, while at church, this memory came rushing back. The beautiful young singer on stage seemed to have discovered my thigh-strangling pants from my teen years. Her parents are apparently much nicer than mine and let her leave the house.

I debated with myself. *Poor thing. Does she realize how skintight those are? Is that what I looked like thirty years ago? Stop it, Joanne, you're being old-fashioned. Those pants are in style again.*

My thoughts were interrupted by my extremely cool seventeen-year-old son. Right in the middle of a worship song, he leaned down and whispered in my ear, "That girl should *not* be wearing those pants." Once again, confirmation that my very own mean mom had been right.

What Does "Mean" Really Mean?

The definition of the word *mean* is to be unkind or malicious. Though you might cringe at being defined this way, it's exactly how your children feel you're behaving when you keep them from what they want, enforce daily chores, or thwart their Friday night plans.

This is the moment the parent-child language barrier begins. You see, a mean mom defines the word *mean* quite a bit differently.

A mean mom keeps her word when it's hard.

A mean mom gives, models, and expects respect.

A mean mom knows her child's friends and where
    they live.

A mean mom instills dinner times, bedtimes,
    and curfews.

A mean mom treads water longer than her child can
    make it rain.

A mean mom never makes excuses for her child's
    strengths or weaknesses.

A mean mom doesn't let her own fears overrule her
    child's freedoms.

A mean mom sees the adult her child can be and inspires
until he or she catches the vision.

A mean mom asks forgiveness for her mistakes.

A mean mom loves passionately, encourages openly, and
behaves righteously.

And if she's married, a mean mom puts her husband
before her child.

My friend and I use "mean mom" as kind of a code
for being a parent when it's hard. —CARRIE SCHMECK

In the context of mean mom, the word *mean* can be defined much differently between mom and child. So begins the expansion of that communication gap you've heard about. What a son or daughter sees as malicious or unkind, a mean mom sees as keeping protective boundaries and inspiring good character traits, so she makes no excuses for uncomfortable situations that are fueled by a loving boundary.

Children don't understand boundaries as being helpful or for their lasting good. Their minds can't wrap around anything more than their immediate wants and needs at this very nanosecond. This is where mean moms dig in and remember they are training each little one to overcome obstacles, never quit, and never, ever give up.

A mean mom's mission statement is this: I'm not raising a child. I'm raising an adult. This mission statement becomes her mantra and reminds her of the ultimate goal: to work herself out of a job.

Marshmallow Mom

When I shared my idea of a mean mom book with a friend, she expressed her concern. "My mom was incredibly mean. Not the *mean* you're talking about. She was so disciplined and hurtful. The scars she's left affect me still. She's the reason I'm such a pushover with my girls today. I tend to be a marshmallow, that's what my kids call me—marshmallow mom. I know I need to be better at keeping boundaries, but I'm so afraid I'll become like my mother that I cave in every time. I don't want my kids to hate me like I hated my mom."

It's sadly true. There are moms who have a genetic mean streak. Oftentimes victims of their own parents' physical or emotional abuse, they pass on discouragement and warped parenting disciplines that mold their children in painful ways.

Let me be very clear here. This is *not* the kind of mean I'm talking about in this book. The mean mom I'm talking about loves her children more than she disciplines them. Joy is what permeates her home, and faith is the foundation and the groundwork she is laying.

Even when a mother is kind, caring, and understanding, she looks mean to her children when she lays down a boundary or rule. What is considered mean in the eyes of a four-year-old is considered wise in the eyes of a forty-four-year-old. This is the kind of mean I mean.

> *A mean mom's mission statement is this: I'm not raising a child. I'm raising an adult.*

"She should've been meaner."

Ask most adults over the age of thirty if their parents were mean, and you'll get lots of different answers. I posed this very question to my girlfriend.

"Yes. I thought my mom was very mean." Gina, a mother of two, answered the question as she cut my hair. "She wouldn't let me stay out late at night and needed to know my friends' first and last names. But, to tell you the truth . . ." She stopped snipping and held her scissors midair. "I don't think she was mean enough." A tiny smile etched her face. "She was actually pretty naïve. She should've been meaner."

New York Times best-selling author Amy Chua, a self-pro-claimed Chinese mean mom, wrote her book *The Battle Hymn of the Tiger Mother* to share her take on Asian mothering and why it works. What she didn't bargain for was the western world's curiosity and national media backlash. Even with the news reports and innu-merable articles chiming in their dislike of her parenting methods, this book shot to the number one biography/memoir ranking and was in the top one hundred books sold on Amazon for quite a while.

Negative press or not, millions of moms bought her book. They want to know how to stand their ground, what parenting hills are worth dying on, and how they too can raise children to become responsible adults who stand a better chance at success. Whether you agree with Chua's parenting style or not, her daughters have played piano at Carnegie Hall, and they are straight-A students. As my husband likes to say, "The proof is in the pudding."

I'm no tiger mom, but I am a self-proclaimed mean mom. I guess you could call me a Christ-Following Bald-Eagle Mom. My children haven't played at Carnegie Hall or won the Nobel Peace Prize, but they have made it to adulthood in one piece. They're responsible and respectful and still call on my birthday and visit on Mother's Day. They've grown up to be productive adults who respect and care for others, and that's even after years of daily chores and paying for their first cars and a big chunk of their col-lege tuition. I'd call that a mean-mom success story.

As you read through each chapter, you'll learn ways to encour-age your kids so that together you can build your child's founda-tion for a successful and God-honoring future. You may laugh out loud about what I share, but silently I think you'll agree. You may believe a few of my parenting techniques are insanity, but secretly I know you'll use them. And, by the time you finish this book, you'll discover what quite a few parents have known for a long, long time—Mean Moms Raise Great Kids.

Mom to Mom

How do you define a mean mom?

A mean mom is a good mom. When a kid calls their mom mean, it confirms Mom has made a rule and stuck to it. —MALEA BAER

A mean mom stands by what she says (no means no) regardless of any whiny manipulation by children. She sticks to her guns even when a child screams "I hate you," and most importantly, she doesn't rescue her children from every bad situation they get themselves into.
—EVA CHRISTIAN

A mean mom cares enough to give her kids boundaries that guide them wisely through life.
—LARA VAN HULZEN

A mean mom means not giving in to every whim of a child who lacks wisdom to know what is best for them. It means not surrendering when they pout, cry, threaten, or withdraw. If the parent waffles in the face of such a challenge, "It's nothing but work, work, work" (to quote the movie *The Princess Bride*). A mean mom must set the foundation and let her children know she won't be manipulated or coerced. Once that's established, parenting is fun! When I was growing up, I could manipulate my parents pretty easily. I know all the tricks and I don't fall for them! —ELIZABETH THOMPSON

CHAPTER TWO

Mean Moms Were Marshmallow Moms

Each of us has a story behind our behavior.
—Valerie E. Hess and Marti Watson Garlett, *Habits of a Child's Heart*

Mean moms come in all shapes and sizes. Did you know marshmallow moms have many different characteristics, too? Most are known to be sugary sweet with a heart as soft as fluffy whipped cream. Think about it. A marshmallow's biggest ingredient is processed sugar. I mean, c'mon . . . who doesn't love a little sugar? You have to admit it's easy to be a pushover in the boundaries department when it comes to our kids.

A mother's love is superhuman. Made up of impenetrable strength, it's miraculously unconditional and lasts longer than life. Yet, this titanium powerhouse of heartfelt emotion is known to melt under nothing more than a child's wants and desires.

Our son, Samuel, was around six years old when he perfected his "boo-boo lip." A few years later, when the Disney movie *Tangled* came out, he discovered another look: "the smolder." Thus, the infamous "smabooboo" was born. A cross between a boo-boo face and a smoldering gaze, it gets me to surrender every time. He's thirteen now, and when he looks at me this way, I'd hand over the car keys if he asked.

Would you like to know a secret? The majority of mean moms are recovering marshmallow moms. Unfortunately, not enough of us are in rehab. Lately, no matter who I meet, I'm surrounded by marshmallows. Maybe you know a few.

A jumbo-sized marshmallow mom is fueled by love, codependence, and a dash of mom-guilt for good measure. She sacrifices her life hourly for her child. Usually a pushover, she takes the shape of the parent her child wants her to be.

Her default answer is *yes* because, after all, she hates to see her child sad. Instead of making tough decisions, she looks to see what her friends are doing and leaves the rest up to her husband. *Go ask your father* are the four most common words you'll hear when she is wrestling with a decision. She boasts, "The children know me so well. I struggle to follow through with discipline. I just can't. I mean, look at those adorable faces!"

> *A jumbo-sized marshmallow mom is fueled by love, codependence, and a dash of mom-guilt for good measure.*

As far as good health is concerned, a marshmallow has no redeeming qualities. Google it, people. Sugar feeds cancer and bad bacteria and is as addictive as any street drug. Being soft and sickly sweet as a mom can affect a child in detrimental ways, too. A mom with a gooey, soft center breeds entitlement, disrespect, laziness, and selfishness, among other unflattering character traits.

The result? This sweet mama fueled by heartfelt intentions is so blinded by love she unknowingly enables unhealthy habits and overlooks bad manners. A sweet marshmallow mom would argue, "There's no limit to what I will do to help my children." This jumbo-sized marshmallow-mommy mission statement, meant to help, cripples her child instead. Her children become idols, and with each passing year, she's that much closer to throwing her own marriage under the bus.

Have I explained you at all? Or maybe you're thinking, *goodness, I'm not jumbo-sized*, and maybe you're not. Maybe you're a mini marshmallow instead. You're one of those cute tiny marshmallows we plop into our kids' cocoa mugs when the first cold weather blows in. I mean, who doesn't love mini marshmallows?

Mini-Marshmallow Moms

Personally, I've always battled my inner mini marshmallow. My biggest struggle is codependency. I come from a long line of codependents who taught me well. If my child can do something, I can do it better and faster—to save them time and lend a helping hand, of course. My intentions are always good.

Most of us fall into the camp of cocoa-sized marshmallows. Tying a child's shoes for far too long, or giving a teenager the summer off instead of encouraging that first job sure seem like kind and tender ways to mother them, but we have to ask ourselves, "Are we helping them in the long run?" A mini-marshmallow mom thinks she is.

There's an area of weakness in a mini-marshmallow mom's parenting skill set. Never a bold or glaring issue, it's the teeny-tiny day-to-day decisions that add up and stunt our child's adult development. Most mini-marshmallow moms encourage their kids to remain kids and soak up every precious moment. I know I did. But what I was really doing was smothering their future independence and hard work lessons in sugary goodness.

The truth is, it's sometimes hard to see where I make mistakes as a mom. But once they're exposed, I can make positive steps forward. Whether you're a jumbo or a mini, maybe you'll see yourself in a few famous marshmallow moms below.

Marshmallow Moms

Maria Mykidcantdothat—She's the grammar-school mom who still ties her son's shoes and the high-school mom who makes her daughter's bed. She sets and clears the dishes each night so her kids can watch TV before bed, and she does the laundry for her teenagers because they just don't understand how to use a washer and dryer like she does. This woman lives by the words, "He can't do that," and "She's still too young." Her greatest complaint? Having her son still living at home after college. Because, after all, at twenty-six years old, he "just can't" find a job in this economy.

Emma Emptythreats—Do you know her? She's a close friend of Robin Repeatsherself50times. These moms stick together. A play-date isn't over until Robin repeats "Put that away. Put that away. Put that away." Emma has her friend's back and follows up with a couple dozen of these: "If you don't put that away . . . if you don't put that away . . . if you don't put that away." How does their one-two parenting punch work? Their children hear only white noise and are trained to ignore every word.

Holly Hasafavorite—"Did you hear about Dillon?" You receive moment-by-moment updates about her golden child: who his friends are, what teacher he has this year, or what he's struggling with this week. She calls you if he makes the football team and texts you if he doesn't. Her mini-marshmallow weakness is encouragement heaped in large doses. Her primary focus is her one child. Except, she has two others she never mentions.

Polly Protector—Second cousin to Hillary Helicopter, Polly corners the market in protective gear. Her daughter wears a bike helmet, knee pads, and floaties in the bathtub. She tries to keep her child safe and thwart any harm that might come her way. She mistakenly believes she stands guard out of parental love when it's really fear that fuels her. Her protective, mama-bear instinct to shield and insulate will teach her child to become an adult who fears, too.

Delia Doestoomuch—Delia just wants to help. Carpool, team mom, PTA, classroom volunteer, Cub Scout leader—the list is long and her day is longer. A pleaser extraordinaire, she raises her hand for any request, big or small. She hasn't puckered up and said the word *no* since 2008. Her soft and gooey center couldn't whisper that word if her life depended on it. She's training her kids to be busy adults, and when they are old they may never depart from it.

Evelyn Everythingisfunny—Evelyn giggles when her toddler calls her by her first name. She laughs harder when her four-year-old shouts the same word her husband used when he stubbed his toe. She takes nothing her child does very seriously because, after all, "He's only two." Evelyn doesn't believe respect is a hill to die on. She thinks this is a lesson her child will learn in time. From the outside world, she seems the most joyful, but the disrespectful adult she's encouraging her child to be will wipe the smile right off her face.

Donna Doasisaynotasido—This mom confuses her kids when it comes to modeling good character and behavior. She uses profanity and shakes her fist when someone cuts her off on the road but reminds her kids that watching movies with foul language isn't okay. She calls in sick to work when she's as healthy as a horse but puts her foot down when her kids want to do the same to work on a school project. She's a hot mess at living a healthy lifestyle but believes her words will override her actions. Donna makes sure to remind them, "Cigarettes can kill you," as she hacks up a lung and blows smoke rings in the air.

Penny Putsthekidsfirst-Everytime—She's a woman who hyphenated her name because she doesn't want to lose her female identity. Ironically, it's her husband who disappears instead.

Motherhood is now her first priority, and she prides herself on raising great kids. Her husband? He moved out three weeks ago. Penny didn't notice until today.

Nancy Notmykid—This is the patron parent of bullies. She's too consumed with her own life to pay attention to what her kid is doing. Never holding her little angel accountable, she raises her child with more freedom than the Liberty Bell. When her son craves a loving boundary or two and acts out for a bit of her attention, she blames the "other kid" every time.

Lucy Lookdownyournose—"Why aren't you breastfeeding? It's been nine years and I still pump and freeze my milk. It's a shame you gave up so soon." Lucy's son was born potty trained. She reminds you of your failings as a mom. Her marshmallow tendency is to allow her child to make his own bedtime and nutrition choices. You'll find her most often around new parents. After all, she's a new mom, too, but she's obviously a lot smarter than you.

Patricia Pinterest—You struggle a lot with Patty. Her home is Pinterest-perfect, created with nothing more than chalkboard paint, sparklers, burlap, and pink cupcakes. When the mere sight of a Mason jar at Walmart makes you break out in a cold sweat, you realize your loathing might need medical attention. It's true, Patty's heart is wrapped up in her home, but it's her kids who desire to be wrapped in her arms instead. With her time and focus on pillows and paints, her kids wish they were one of her projects.

Do you recognize a few of these marshmallow mamas? You might be wondering, *How does she know my friends?* They were easy to introduce because quite a few of them have been me. I'm a recovering old softy and I've struggled with prioritizing marriage and family life. I understand how difficult it is to change, especially if you've been leaning on poor parenting examples around you, but it's still possible. After all, how do you eat an elephant? One small bite at a time.

Parental Employment

At the height of diapers and Desitin, I remember quite a few over-whelming years. As a new mom, I underestimated the colossal life change a baby brings. There was a time I mistakenly believed a child would be a pretty accessory to the life I was already living—a tiny, dimpled mom-bling to wear with my favorite outfit and make my life whole.

I couldn't have been more wrong.

My rock bottom came one morning as the odiferous scent of spit-up and sweet potatoes permeated the air—the organic body spray of motherhood. Exhausted after changing the fortieth diaper that day, I slumped down at my kitchen table and dropped my face into my hands.

Tears welled as I prayed silently. *Really, Lord, is this my lot in life? Teaching children to put away their toys? Reminding them over and over to say kind words? Disciplining them when they don't share? Everything I seem to do is wrong and if you haven't noticed, they are the problem, not me. Father, aren't you aware I'm wiping tiny bums and tinier noses—seven days a week, twenty-four hours a day? Lord, surely you must have something bigger and, well, maybe more important for me to be doing with my life.*

God's holy message came from a woman in our church. After I whined to her about yet another frustrating day, she gently said, "Don't despise the days of small beginnings."

Do not despise these small beginnings, for the LORD rejoices to see the work begin, to see the plumb line in Zerubbabel's hand. (Zech. 4:10 NLT)

The same words can be said of changing our parenting style. I'll be the first to admit, her words both stung and encouraged me. I knew the Scripture. In this Bible story, Zechariah encourages Zerubbabel to finish rebuilding the temple—a gargantuan task that had its beginnings in less monumental ways.

Charles Spurgeon gives hope to parents everywhere: "God accepts your little works if they are done in faith in his dear Son. God will give success to your little works: God will educate you by your little works to do greater works; and your little works may call out others who shall do greater works by far than ever you shall be able to accomplish."[2]

On one hand, I felt bad complaining about my children. Apparently, I was more of the problem than they were. On the other hand, my friend gave me the ability to start looking at small things in light of the bigger picture. Each tiny opportunity was meant for God's purpose. Zechariah was encouraging Zerubbabel's holy work, too. God's work has the power to transform all involved. These child-rearing years would be sanctification in my life. I began to see my parenting role as a God-honoring employment opportunity.

This conversation opened my eyes to needed changes and gave me confidence that I was given a job to accomplish. Which made tweaking a few of my marshmallow-mom tendencies much easier. Author and missionary Elisabeth Elliot says in her book *Passion and Purity*, "The God who created names and numbers the stars in the heavens also numbers the hairs of my head. He pays attention to very big things and to very small ones. What matters to me matters to Him, and that changes my life."[1]

Small Beginnings—Bigger End Results

Marshmallow moms don't change overnight. It's the small things, the tiny beginnings that mold and shape us to be the parents our children need most. Charles Spurgeon gives hope to parents everywhere: "God accepts your little works if they are done in faith in his dear Son. God will give success to your little works: God will educate you by your little works to do greater works; and your little works may call out others who shall do greater works by far than ever you shall be able to accomplish."[2]

> Teach your child to pick up her toys and you raise a
> responsible adult.
> Teach your child to share and you raise a kind adult.
> Teach your child to choose words carefully and you raise
> an encouraging adult.
> Teach your child to serve and you raise a sacrificial adult.
> Teach your child patience and you raise an adult who
> knows peace.
> Teach your child about hard work by experiencing hard
> work and you raise an adult who won't go hungry.
> Teach your child about heartache and you raise an adult
> who has joy in any storm.
> Teach your child not to fear and you raise an adult who
> can face any adventure life brings.
> Teach your child to value differences and you raise an
> adult who respects all people.
> Teach your child to be happy with little and you raise an
> adult who is content.
> Teach your child all the reasons *you* love God and you
> raise an adult who may desire to love God, too.

Even if you're known by your friends as *Nancy Notmykid* or *Donna Doasisaynotasido*, each small step away from a bad habit is one big step toward a good one. Be strong and courageous, mom. Whether you are a mini marshmallow or the squishiest jumbo-sized marshmallow mom on the planet, today is the beginning of your mean mom journey.

No matter what small thing you are doing, no matter what itty-bitty something you do for the umpteenth time this week, stand strong and remember—small beginnings are holy work in your children's lives. As you change, you are building an immovable foundation for their change and the plans God has for your adult children one day.

Mom to Mom

Do you struggle with your inner "marshmallow mom"?

℮ I'm a peacemaker by nature, which is the source of my inner marshmallow mom. I. Just. Want. Peace—NO MATTER WHAT. So, I often fight the tendency to give in or be soft for the sake of sanity. When I think of my mom friends who are more vigilant about certain aspects of motherhood like discipline, healthy eating, teaching responsibility, etc., I'm inspired to abandon my desire for 'peace' for the sake of raising great kids.

—JESSICA WOLSTENHOLM

℮ I fight being a marshmallow because what my kids don't understand is giving in that one time puts us back to square one. So I have to stand firm, even if I don't really want to. —ERIKA HRANICKY

  As my daughter has gotten older, I find it harder and harder not to soften when she's angry with me. When she was a toddler it was easy. But now that she's thirteen years old and we're closer, I find myself second guessing myself and wondering, *Am being too harsh?* I really soften if she self-criticizes. While I don't want to reward her with attention when she's critical of herself, I also want to keep her self-esteem up. My hope is this is a small phase and we will grow together. —KRISTINE MOUL

Notes

[1] Elisabeth Elliot, *Passion and Purity* (Old Tappan, NJ: Revell, 1984).

[2] Charles Spurgeon, quoted in David Guzik, "Zechariah 4 – By My Spirit, Says the LORD," Enduring Word Media Online Commentary, www.enduringword.com/commentaries/3804.htm.

CHAPTER THREE

Mean Moms Walk by Faith

If you want to change the children, change the parent.
Any growth plan for your family must begin with you.
—John Maxwell, *The 15 Invaluable Laws of Growth*

Before we race headfirst into parenting the *mean mom* way, it's important to understand what this type of mom looks like. Who is she? What makes her tick? I've met quite a few great examples of motherhood over the years, and the one thing I've noticed the majority of these women have in common is their unwavering faith in God.

Mean moms and marshmallow moms alike are going to need much more than positive thinking to make it through the parenting years. Why? Parenting is incredibly hard, and we need supernatural help. If thinking positively were enough, then I'd be able to positively think myself into size five jeans, too. As a Christ-following bald-eagle mom, I can't point you to parenting successes without sharing about the very One who gives me mine: Jesus.

Call me a spiritual late bloomer. I was thirty-one years old and already a mommy of two when I surrendered my life to Jesus

Christ. Surprisingly, one of the many stepping stones that brought me to this decision was a late-night infomercial for worship music on a dozen CDs with more songs about God than I knew what to do with. Singer and songwriter Bob Carlisle was the spokesperson and, well, anyone who sang "Butterfly Kisses" was a friend of mine and out came my credit card.

It was the first time I spent money to purposely listen to music about God. These songs spoke right to me. The CDs played when I cleaned the kitchen and ran errands in the car and anywhere else I could slide them in and pump up the volume. "Two Sets of Joneses" by the group Big Tent Revival became one of my favorites. My children heard it so often, it became their favorite, too. Meghan, my oldest of four children, sang it a cappella at her public school talent show in fourth grade.

Two couples with the last name of Jones. The difference? One has a relationship with Jesus and the other doesn't. This cautionary tale ends with heartache for the couple who founded their relationship on each other and worldly treasures, or—as the Bible defines it—a foundation of sand, while the couple who has a relationship with Christ founded their life on him—the rock. No matter what life brings their way, at the end of the song they're still standing.

Right behavior will always follow right beliefs. Never the other way around. —MICHAEL YOUSSEF

Therefore whoever hears these sayings of Mine, and does them, I will liken him to a wise man who built his house on the rock: and the rain descended, the floods came, and the winds blew and beat on that house; and it did not fall, for it was founded on the rock.

> But everyone who hears these sayings of Mine, and
> does not do them, will be like a foolish man who built
> his house on the sand: and the rain descended, the
> floods came, and the winds blew and beat on that house;
> and it fell. And great was its fall. (Matt. 7:24–27 NKJV)

Before I lead you any further down the road of parenting with loving boundaries, there's something very important you need to know. A foundation makes a difference.

Without an incredibly strong foundation, any house—from your own to Buckingham Palace—would easily crumble. Or, as Big Tent Revival asks us in "Two Sets of Joneses": Is your life built on the rock of Christ Jesus or on a sandy foundation you've managed to lay?

Precious mom-friend, I ask you to keep this in mind as we travel through these chapters together. A foundation in Christ changed me from the inside out. Jesus is real and alive, and God's word is the unmovable rock you need when raising children.

I wouldn't be able to do this "Mom" thing if it weren't for Jesus. —JOY WILLIAMSON

Changed to Be Their Example

I was working a graveyard shift as a 9-1-1 dispatcher when, during the wee hours of the early morning, God used my supervisor to question me about my faith, or lack thereof. At the time, I was going through a divorce and was a single mom of two. When you work twelve-hour shifts together, day in and day out, you talk about pretty much everything, so it was only a matter of time before God was on topic.

In between emergency calls, my eyes heavy, he asked, "How do you know you're going to heaven?"

Everyone at the police department knew Randy was a former missionary in Ireland before he took the job as our new supervisor of emergency communications. He was fun and kind. We never took offense when he brought up his faith. So I thought I'd play along. He'd asked me my thoughts on God before. I came to realize I didn't know as much as I thought I did about Jesus.

How do I know I'm going to heaven? What an easy question, I thought. "Because I'm a good person." *Duh.* "I'm nice to everyone and I've never murdered anybody." I smiled back. *I'll take Bible knowledge for $300, Mr. Trebek.*

"Sin is sin, Joanne. No sin is worse than another."

Did he just call me a sinner? Now I was awake. "Go on."

"God is holy. A holy God is sinless, perfect. Sin can't be in his presence."

"What does that have to do with Jesus?" I prodded. Being raised in a traditional church, I thought I knew all the answers. I wanted to hear more.

"Think of it this way. If I had two buckets of crystal-clear water and dumped a cup of thick, black crude oil in one of the buckets and only a dropper full of crude oil in the other and stirred, which one is tainted?"

"Both," I answered quietly.

"Exactly. Sin is sin. It can't be in the presence of a holy God. Whether you murder or tell a lie, it's sin."

Randy must have seen his explanation coming into focus for me. "I'm a sinner?"

He encouraged me. "We all are. But Jesus died for your sins and mine. A spotless, sinless lamb gave his life as a sacrifice for ours so we can have a relationship with a holy God. All we have to do is ask."

I wasn't tired anymore. He had my full attention. "Would you like to pray with me?" He smiled.

Was he serious? Did he really just ask me to pray with him? In my police uniform, tethered with a headset like an umbilical cord to a monitor? With my girlfriends in the room? Thank you very much, but no thank you.

Randy beautifully shared the gospel story with me that morning. Then he wrote down a few Scripture verses on a slip of paper. "Read these when you have a minute." He smiled. It was the very first time I'd recognized myself as a sinner in need of a savior. Which brought to mind the second issue—I absolutely knew I'd never asked God for forgiveness or asked Jesus to be Lord of my life. Needless to say, I drove home from work very carefully that morning.

If we want to raise godly children, the best way to achieve this is to be godly parents. —RAY COMFORT

Later, in the quiet of my home, I searched to find a Bible in my house, dusted it off, pulled out that slip of paper, and looked each verse up.

Romans 3:10	Romans 3:23
Romans 5:12	Romans 6:23
Romans 5:8	Romans 10:13
Romans 10:9–10	

Moments later, on the office floor of my house and in tears, I surrendered my life to Jesus. Change was inevitable.

When I got up off my knees, I didn't feel any different. Yet with each passing day, a difference in me became apparent. I hungered for God and his Word. I experienced my first home Bible study when Randy and his wife, Cindy, offered to come over each week. Later, I began attending a good Bible-teaching church and loved it.

A mean mom knows we will answer to God one day when he asks, "What did you do with what I gave you?" When it comes to raising godly kids, I want to hear him say, "Well done." —MICHELLE BUSCHINI

It's Not a Religion—It's a Relationship

I recoil at being called *religious*. That word reminds me of cold statues and legalistic traditions. I am in a relationship. It just so happens that relationship is with the One true, living God.

My husband and I are in a relationship and make a point to spend as much time together as possible. So why wouldn't I clear my schedule to spend a little time in my most important relationship—with Jesus? He is living water to my parched soul. Spiritual hydration means I'll be able to go that extra mama-mile. So, what does all of this have to do with being a mean mom or even a marshmallow mom? A lot.

When you need wisdom or those tough parenting times come (and they will), they're a lot easier to navigate when the One who created our kids has a relationship with you and me.

Do You Spend Time with Jesus?

"Quiet time? Really? Sheesh, I wish."

Ever uttered those words out loud? Or maybe you were the one silently screaming them in your head the last time your girlfriend shared how well her daily time with God was going. Either way, I get you and so do a lot of other moms.

I'm going to let you off the hook today. It's not about a specific time of day or number of hours reading your Bible. It's not about raising your hand for every Beth Moore study or being prostrate in prayer longer than an Italian monk. Nope. Quiet time looks different for each of us. It's set apart, intentional time with Jesus. Period.

For those of you not well versed in "Christianese": quiet time is the same as devotion time or spending a few minutes meditating over a Scripture verse. It's a spiritual refueling for your day.

The moment you tell Jesus you are his, the very second you know that he is real and alive, you are in a relationship with him. As with any relationship, the way you learn about him and wholly trust him is to get to know him. No better way to sanctify our lives alongside his than by spending time with him.

"But what if I don't have time?"

Remember, there's no condemnation in Christ Jesus (Rom. 8:1). God understands when you're making breakfast for the kids, or taking that extra shift at work, or running errands for your husband. Unless you're purposely trading your time with him for quiet time with the Kardashians, don't beat yourself up. He is a merciful and loving God.

Need a Little Time? Ask For It

When my children were babies, it was difficult to make time. I had the best intentions. I even kept a Bible and a devotion book in the bathroom. I figured the Lord didn't care where we spent time together, only that we did.

I remember complaining to a woman at church, "I just don't have time. I've tried. My mornings are full of kids and a whole lot of crazy. How do you do it?"

"I ask him for it."

"Say again?"

"I ask him for it. When my days are busy and I don't think I'll have time, I ask the Lord to give me a little. Sure enough, he does—every time." She winked.

When I first asked God to open up my daily calendar for a little *us* time, I thought it mere coincidence when the children took a longer nap. By the third and fourth time I silently asked him for a few stolen moments, it was clear he was orchestrating our time together. It never failed. Every time I opened his Word, I read a little something I could hang on to just for me. Why was I surprised? Who better to mold and shape time than the very One who created time and whose eternal existence is not bound by it?

A parent's main task is to receive a child as a charge from the Lord and then to dedicate the child to God's ways. —RICK JOHNSON

If you're in a difficult season for quiet time, consider the following ways to squeeze a little spiritual togetherness into each day.

- The Daily Audio Bible. Here's an app I love, from dailyaudiobible.com. Remember, faith comes by hearing and hearing by the Word of God. In a hurry? Put on your makeup and hit play. Listen as Genesis to Revelation is read aloud.
- Or maybe you'd rather read a Psalm and a Proverb a day.

- Have you ever considered the chronological Bible? It's a great way to read God's Word from cover to cover in the order the events occurred. It brings God's story to life.
- Keep a devotion book in the bathroom. Charles Spurgeon might be a little offended to know how much time he's spent in mine. There are days moms go one hundred miles an hour. Devotion books strategically placed around the house are priceless.
- Digital downloads. Listen to messages from favorite pastors with a smartphone. (This is my personal choice for inspiration doing cardio time on a treadmill.)
- Email. Sign up for a daily devotion. Most ministry websites have a slice of godly wisdom and encouragement to help you focus on the Lord. Take advantage of one or two or twelve.

Before you attempt to parent on your own, filling up first is a good idea. By the time you tuck your last little munchkin into bed, I promise you'll be grateful you did.

A God of Loving Boundaries

Mean moms are infamous for boundaries. We make them and keep them. *Loving boundaries—* two words that remind me of every single day of my parenting journey. They are often seen as *mean* by a child or a teenager. I use them to protect my children and guide them into adulthood. It would be a disservice to write a book about *parenting with loving boundaries* without pointing to the perfect example—God himself.

> *Mean moms are infamous for boundaries. We make them and keep them.*

God is our Father; "to all who did receive him, to those who believed in his name, he gave the right to become children of God— children born not of natural descent, nor of human decision or a husband's will, but born of God" (John 1:12–13). He is the creator of heaven and earth and each one of us. Once we acknowledge his son and believe in his saving grace, we become his child. Boundaries are a tool he used from the beginning to shape the world we live in today.

In Genesis, we see the creation story unfold. The Lord separates light from darkness, day from night, and land from the waters. Singer and songwriter Nicole C. Mullen reminds us of Job 38:11–12 in her hit song "My Redeemer Lives."

Who taught the sun where to stand in the morning?
And who told the ocean you can only come this far?

I'm grateful God put the ocean in its place. I'm not a good swimmer. I appreciate the opportunity to raise my children on dry land.

Creation boundaries are the first example of God's hand making a limit line for nature. As we read on further in the Old Testament, light and darkness in the form of day and night, along with specific places in our world set apart for land and sea, are just a few examples of how God begins his earthly boundary keeping. Eventually, we come to know the personal loving boundaries he sets up for his children.

The Ten Commandments are familiar to most of humanity. A command is a declaration by a king—a boundary set in place by our loving Father. As we see in Genesis 2, God explains to Adam what he can and can't eat: "GOD took the Man and set him down in the Garden of Eden to work the ground and keep it in order. GOD commanded the Man, 'You can eat from any tree in the garden, except from the Tree-of-Knowledge-of-Good-and-Evil. Don't eat from it. The moment you eat from that tree, you're dead'" (Gen. 2:15–17 *The Message*).

Why would God keep Adam from this tree? Why this boundary? The answer comes a few verses later when we watch the serpent deceive Eve and she partakes of the fruit. Sin is birthed in that moment. God's one line in the sand is crossed, and a loving Father ushers his two children out of Eden to protect them. Why? If they were to eat from the second tree, the Tree of Life, they would die in their sin, eternally hopeless.

There are consequences when boundaries are crossed. Recently, a semitrailer carrying tons of fuel drove over the center divide on the freeway and crashed into cement columns holding up an overpass by our home, exploding into flames and killing the driver. We understand the rules of the road, and the hazards if we don't obey. We know they're put in place for our safety. Still, our children won't always understand.

Try explaining to a three-month-old why a nap is a good idea, or try to explain to your teenager why he has a 10 P.M. curfew. Both conversations can be just as futile. In each case parents are laying a few loving boundaries, and there's probably going to be some pushback when the child doesn't understand why.

A mean mom understands her biggest hurdle is to stand no matter what comes her way. How does she do that? By standing on the only foundation that will give her a firm footing. Faith is what carries her through. Christ holds her up when she wants to quit. Mean moms never have to parent alone because, as I like to say, "One with God is the majority."

Mom to Mom

How do you make time for God each day?

❧ I was horrible at reading my Bible consistently. So, I started reading through the Bible with a group this year on Facebook, and it's helped tremendously, and I've kept on track. —ERYN CREUSERE

❧ One thing I learned to do with my devotion time is to change my expectations. Devotion time is not the same after having children and that's okay. Sometimes I read my Bible as I dry my hair. Other times, it's before the kids get up, or while my children are playing at my feet. I make a point to find God in the midst of the chaos. —LINDSEY BELL

❧ My time with Jesus is so important to make it through my day. I get up at four every morning for quiet time. Otherwise it doesn't happen. —RACHAEL MCKINNEY

❧ A dear friend invited me to participate in the Good Morning Girls Bible Study this fall. This was just what I needed and still need. Now I am using the YouVersion app to read the Bible through in a year, thanks to my amazing husband! My kids are growing up learning a lot more about God than I ever did. —KRISTINE RASO

CHAPTER FOUR

Mean Moms Put Marriage First

Give your children the luxury of seeing one parent who loves the other unconditionally. This will serve them well when they face the challenges of marriage themselves. Give your mate a place of honor in your home.

—Connie Grigsby

W ho is your parenting partner? It's of vital importance. A strong marriage means a strong mean mom. Do your children see a united front? Is their father your first priority or your last? Even the best mean moms can fall into the fatal parent trap: putting kids before their marriage. Do you resemble marshmallow mom Penny Putsthekidsfirst-Everytime? You've put the kids before your husband for so long, he said "so long."

If your kids are numero uno in your life, take heart. I have a few important lessons I learned the hard way. Let's peek into the book of Genesis again. "God said, 'It's not good for the Man to be alone; I'll make him a helper, a companion'" (Gen. 2:18 *The Message*). The first marriage in all of humanity was born: a union between male and female brought together for two reasons, to help one another and bring glory to God.

Adam and Eve's *how we met* story begins beautifully but ends tragically. Neither Eve nor Adam were much of a *help* to the other; instead, they were partners in sin. Sadly, their behavior breaks God's heart and gives them an eviction notice from the Garden of Eden. And reading on, their parenting struggles were more intense than any I've experienced. After all, Cain murders Abel. We aren't given a glimpse into how this grief may have traumatized their parents or their marriage. It makes me wonder if Adam and Eve ever learned to help or support one another. The Bible doesn't give us any hope this was the case.

Paul and I remind our children often, "There's no greater decision you'll make than who you choose to marry." Why is my relationship with my husband so important? It's extremely important, because a family is only as strong as the marriage inside it.

When your marriage is impenetrable, it's a mighty fortress to be reckoned with. Still, there are a few fortress walls I've been known to break down with my own hands. For me, it begins in my head.

> *Marriage does not demand perfection, but it must be given priority.* —H. NORMAN WRIGHT

Dwell There—Take Thoughts Captive

"He is such a slob." "Why can't he think of me for once?" "If he changes the channel one more time, I'm going to scream!"

If you've been married for more than a day and a half, you've probably had some annoying thoughts bounce around in your head. But is negative thinking where your mind camps? Is this the warm dwelling place you've invited negativity to hang out every day?

When we allow our mind to replay hurts and every tiny indiscretion, we create a dwelling place of discouragement for our hearts to live in. Being married isn't easy. It takes daily work. Here's a tip: if you ever meet someone who tells you, "Our marriage is perfect," run. They're lying.

No one leaves the altar for their honeymoon thinking, *Yeah, I've got this.* And if they do, they're quickly schooled that they don't. Take it from someone who has been divorced. I know just how fast those little irritations magically become divorce papers. But here's some good news I'd like to share with you. I didn't understand it years ago, and it begins with a question: What are you dwelling on?

When you think about your husband, what are the first thoughts that come to mind? Close your eyes and take a moment. I'll wait ...

When you think about your husband, what are the first thoughts that come to mind? Close your eyes and take a moment. I'll wait ...

What is your mind's dwelling place? Where are your thoughts most comfortable camping out? Have you decorated your head with discouragement and wrong thinking about your husband?

God's Word reminds me how I should be thinking about my husband, Paul.

"Finally, brothers and sisters, whatever is true, whatever is noble, whatever is right, whatever is pure, whatever is lovely, whatever is admirable—if anything is excellent or praiseworthy—think about such things" (Phil. 4:8–9).

The Greek word for "think about such things" is *logizomai*. It's a verb that means to reckon, to purpose, to account, to weigh, to practice, and (my favorite) to dwell. Tell me: What thoughts are rattling around in that pretty little head of yours? If they're less than encouraging—be intentional. Each thought about your husband is a seed you plant for future harvest.

The more selective you are with seeds, the more delighted you will be with the crop. —MAX LUCADO[1]

Where have you staked out your farmland to plant those seeds? Why don't you try living in the land of encouraging truths about your husband? Here are a few of mine.

> My husband loves me.
> He loves our children.
> He supports my ideas and goals.
> He works very hard to keep a roof over our heads.

If you're an overachiever, why don't you make these thoughts specific? Here's my example.

> He puts out my vitamins on the bathroom sink
>   every morning and every night.
> He pays our bills and doesn't complain about it.
> He tells me I'm beautiful.
> He holds my hand in the car.

Philippians 4:8–9 is truth serum to a hurting relationship. Like I said, no marriage is perfect. I could just as easily have made a list about my husband's shortcomings, and he could do the same about me. But I choose not to. If you need a daily reminder of Philippians

4:8–9, write it down on a yellow sticky note and put it on your bathroom mirror. I've done that before.

Whatever fills our minds will come out in our actions and decisions. —MICHAEL YOUSSEF[2]

Every mean mom needs help. You can't do it alone. Your husband is your parenting partner; he has your back and you have his. Don't be fooled. There is no greater feather in Satan's cap than to destroy your marriage. Your marriage is a beautiful picture of Christ and the church. Now, put those pictures all over the world and give them motion—can you imagine how much a godly marriage infuriates the enemy of our souls?

Would you like to make a difference for the kingdom of God today? Love your husband. Take your thoughts captive and abide in Philippians 4:8–9—a stone fortress of truth. Whatever is positively true about your man—make that your mind's dwelling place and live there.

Are You a Blessing or a Burden?

The ref blew the final whistle and parents cheered our victory, while Paul and I cheered for a much different reason. It was the last day of soccer season. With three of our four kids in soccer that year, it was a day worthy of rejoicing.

But, before we could get too excited, there was still the team party to attend. I'd printed off a coupon that would give us two large pizzas for twenty dollars. Unfortunately, when my husband made his way through the long line of families at Mountain Mike's Pizza, he was told by the gal at the register, "Your total is thirty-eight dollars."

"What?" Paul was taken aback, and I was beckoned with a head nod and a fast wave of his hand. "I thought you said this was going to be only twenty bucks, Joanne."

"Oh, no! I left the coupon in the car," I told him, already heading toward the parking lot.

"Don't bother getting it. Do you see how long this line is? I'm not about to make these people wait for us." He was frustrated.

It didn't help matters when two hours later we were at the grocery store where I'd thought we were eligible for a free turkey. When the clerk charged us for the turkey and explained how I'd confused the deal they were having, my husband was fit to be tied.

As you can imagine, I was not having a very good day and neither was he. When we discussed the incidents later, I apologized, and he shared, "I'm having a hard time seeing where you helped me today. You are making mistakes that create a financial burden for me. I know you didn't do anything intentionally, but these kinds of things are happening a lot lately."

He was right. Lately I wasn't focused on ways I could help him. Sure, I kept the house picked up and made his lunch from time to time, but how was I intentionally trying to make his life easier?

Remember what we talked about at the beginning of this chapter? "Then the LORD God said, 'It is not good for the man to be alone. I will make a helper who is just right for him'" (Gen. 2:18 NLT).

God's Word tells me I was created not only to be Paul's friend but to be a help to him as well. When Paul shared how I created a burden for him instead, I felt terrible. And, I admit, there were a few tears. He is my best friend. I want his life to be easier when I'm a part of it, not more difficult. It got me thinking: How can I be a help to him? As his wife, I shouldn't be his burden-maker; I should be a bearer of his blessings.

I thought I'd share a few ways I've learned to be the blessing and helper God intentionally created me to be.

Follow-through. It's time I became a woman of my word and began to tackle a few of those tasks I personally despise, like cleaning out the kids' closets and my pantry and finishing the laundry. After all, he was thrilled when I organized our silverware drawer. I'm sure he'd be elated to discover his socks all in one place again.

Focus. Quite often I give my husband only one ear when he's talking to me. It's frustrating for him to share a story when I ask him to repeat himself over and over again. Focus. It helps me remember coupons in the car and read the fine print about turkey sales at the grocery store.

Find. Find ways to help. Each morning, I try to ask two powerful questions: "What can I do to help you today?" and "How can I pray for you today?" You'll be amazed to discover how much your husband appreciates these questions. Putting your man first is a powerful marriage-booster.

Fill. My words can be life-giving when I fill my mouth with inspiration and encouragement. There is nothing more taxing on a husband than a wife who nitpicks and complains. I need to fill my husband's ears with life-giving words.

Fun. When Paul wants to relax and have fun, I want to be who he thinks of first. For fun I take him out for a coffee date, or walk into his office to give him a kiss and a cuddle. I've been known to leave a loving message on a sticky note somewhere on his office desk. I've even surprised him with ice cream and a movie in bed.

So many families are struggling to keep their financial heads above the rising economic tide. It's no surprise money is one of the biggest stressors in a marriage. Whether your husband is sensitive to finances in your home or a new job situation, or is just overworked and mentally stretched to his limit, you have the potential to be his biggest help. Don't forget, you're the one God created to stand shoulder to shoulder with him to carry the load together.

Mean Moms and PDA—
Public Display of Affection

When your child is witness to a smooch or two, you may receive a loud dissent—but don't be fooled. It's also a comfort. It reinforces security that you love each other. It's an encouraging sign to a child. Paul and I enjoy making our kids gag every once in a while. If that's not your style, I highly encourage you to show a little G-rated affection when your son or daughter is around.

Paul and I created a favorite game when our four were younger: Red Light–Green Light. While on a drive, we pucker up at every red light. The rule is: a green light gets a pass. Green lights are much appreciated by our kids. As we begin this game, God seems to play along and always gives us more red lights than normal. The best part of red light–green light? Approaching a yellow light. Paul slows way down to hit the red. All the while, a chorus of four children in pain chimes in from the back seats, reminding us of their disgust.

"Oh no—not again."

"God, please help us all!"

"I think I just threw up in my mouth."

"Oh, it burns. It burns. Make them stop!"

Children feel safe and secure in a family where mom and dad show affection from time to time. —JOANNE KRAFT

My own parents set the PDA bar pretty high. I have memories of Mom and Dad sharing lots of kisses and cuddles. Dad was known to chase Mom around the house to steal a kiss. Her laughter is a memory I'll never forget. After dinner, it was common for him to pull Mom onto his lap for a kiss and thank her for a good meal. That was forty years ago. Children don't forget those things.

Here's a bit of mean mom wisdom for the ages: there's no greater gift you can give your kids than to love their father.Keep those negative thoughts in check. Be intentional when you talk about him to the children. You are your husband's blessing, not his burden. Be affectionate toward him in the presence of your kids. Remind yourself daily, "What my children see in our marriage today, I may see one day in theirs."

When I'm dead and gone, my kids may have a lot to say about me. But one thing's for sure—they will know I loved their Dad. My daughter Grace asked me just the other day, "Mom, how long do you want to live?"

Here's a bit of mean mom wisdom for the ages: there's no greater gift you can give your kids than to love their father.

"One day less."

"I know, I know. One day less than Dad." She smiled. I pulled her in for a hug. She was right.

Do you want to know the most powerful support system to mean-mom mothering? A strong relationship with your child's father and their heavenly Father. It's the solid foundation you can lean on every time.

Mom to Mom

What do you love about your husband?

What I love about my husband? He is completely devoted to me and our marriage. Completely. He jokes that if I ever loaded up the car and tried to leave, he'd be right behind me, chasing me down. I would never be rid of him and I'd never want to be. The second thing I love? He would lay down his very life for the gospel of Jesus Christ. —ELAINE OLSEN

℮ Fighting just isn't worth it. Does it drive me crazy after twenty-one years he still loads the dishwasher wrong? Yes. But am I going to fight about it? No. I remind myself, "Is this the hill you want to die on?"
—MELANIE PAETOW

℮ My husband is a dedicated provider who puts his family first. If we need to solve a disagreement about our kids, we discuss it first between us and don't "side" with one child over our spouse. —SUSAN PANZICA

℮ My husband is an amazing servant-hearted man who challenges me to be better every single day. The glue that keeps us together is humility and flexibility.
—JESSICA WOLSTENHOLM

Notes

[1] *The Complete Guide to Christian Quotations* (Uhrichsville, OH: Barbour Publishers, 2011), 308.

[2] Ibid., 309.

CHAPTER FIVE

Mean Moms Pray

Until you know that life is war,
you cannot know what prayer is for.
—John Piper

*C*all it mother's intuition, call it logic, but I believe it was divine intervention—I knew without a doubt my daughter had jumped in.

Running toward the crowd of bathing suit-clad people, I pushed and shoved, squeezing myself in front of at least a hundred people in the sultry Texas heat—daring anyone to stop me. Finally reaching the very front of the line, I yelled to the attendant, "I need to jump in. My little girl might be out there." He gave the coveted head nod, and in seconds a huge wave came roaring toward me, launching me into the not-so-Lazy River ride.

Like a snake, the Lazy River wound its way through the amusement park, carrying me in its current. Exits were peppered throughout—that is, if you were strong enough to make your way to them. A grown man couldn't stand in place—the current is much too strong. At about four feet deep, it wasn't possible our five-year-old could touch the bottom without going under. My eyes scanned the surface for a bobbing blonde ponytail. People quickly floated by, bumping up against me on a freeway of colorful blow-up alligators, lions, and inflatable chairs. I could barely breathe, trying not to think of the possibility my baby girl was trapped beneath one.

A few years earlier, Grace went missing for a few minutes after she ran off to chase seagulls on the beach. When I'd found her, a woman who'd helped in the search gently took me aside and put her arm around me. "I know it's tough to focus when something like this happens. But these are the moments you must stop and pray." Her wisdom rang in my ears as I searched once again for my daughter.

I could hardly think, let alone pray. But I needed God's help. *Put your angels around her, Lord. Put your angels around her, Father. Please put your angels around her.* Over and over I whispered the prayer and mantra of a frantic mother who had lost her child—while battling the urge to collapse and cry.

If our children get lost, they've been taught to look for a grandma-figure for help, someone with tender eyes, soft hugs, and a caring way about them. Would my daughter remember what we'd taught her?

Making my way around to the end, panic set in. Where was she? The Fourth of July crowd seemed to have grown larger. I began to lose hope.

Then I spotted her.

About fifty yards from me, she stood like a drowned rat, stray golden locks pasted to her flushed face. An older woman was comforting her, wrapping her in an embrace. Even at a distance, I could see my little girl was crying. My daughter had found a grandma.

I ran to them and dropped to my knees, throwing my arms around my wet little love. Her tears flowed freely now, while I cooed in her ear, "Gracie, you're okay, honey. I'm right here. Don't cry, sweetheart." I looked up at the deep wrinkled face of our little girl's rescuer. "You're an angel," I whispered to this stranger.

Looking up into the warm eyes of Grace's hero, my voice shaky, I said, "I asked God to put angels around her. You're an answer to prayer."

To me, she was an angel in the sense that she'd been the helping hands and divine answer to my anxious prayers that day. The older woman smiled at me. "Your daughter was struggling in the current. I reached out to help her and—"

My husband interrupted our reunion to scoop Grace up into his arms. Somehow in this bulging holiday crowd, he'd found us. I was almost as relieved as our daughter was. A group hug was in order. Remembering our rescuer and my manners, I turned back around to begin introductions.

"Paul, this is the woman who found Gra—" but she was no longer there. Where had she gone? I was disappointed she'd walked away before we could talk more.

Later that night, Grace cuddled up beside me outside on a blanket. We sat together eating BBQ and watching fireworks explode in the purple night sky. She shared with me a little more about this woman who had snatched her out of the water. "Mommy, when she helped me she told me not to be afraid. She asked me my name, and when I told her it was Grace, she said, 'Your name is Grace because the grace of God is with you.'"

My breath caught in my throat.

It was clear to me now. Our daughter's hero hadn't walked away. She wasn't swallowed up by the Fourth of July crowd. An angel had been sent to help us—clothed in the body of a grandma. My frantic-mama prayers were heard and answered. God's grace poured out on our Grace who once was lost but now was found.

> Let us therefore come boldly to the throne of grace, that we may obtain mercy and find grace to help in time of need. (Heb. 4:16 NKJV)

Mean Mom Communication on Steroids

To converse with God is communication on steroids. Prayer is an element of my faith that has grown over the years. It's also, I believe, as a Christ-following mean mom, the piece of my spiritual heritage I can underestimate most. Prayer doesn't always change my situation. It doesn't always change the person I'm praying for. But prayer always changes me. It opens my eyes to see my struggle differently—with a big slice of God's perspective.

There's a misunderstanding I hear among a lot of mean and marshmallow moms alike. They believe they're falling short if they're not setting aside hours a day to step inside their prayer closet and pour their hearts out for their family and friends. Emily, a mother of three young children, shared, "My days are a blur. I fall into bed exhausted and remember a million things I didn't do with my kids. Prayer is always one of them."

Hear me out. I've said it before. Please don't think this way. The apostle Paul reminds us in the Book of Romans to stop condemning ourselves (8:1). If Jesus resides in us, guilt is no more. God's mercies are new every day. Lord willing, you'll have another chance to open your eyes and ask God to guide your day tomorrow.

*Someone once said, when we work we work,
but when we pray God works.* —BILL HYBELS

God's grace is overflowing. It's an abundant gift of unmerited favor bestowed on his children—us. Prayer included. Would you consider your son a failure and withhold your love if he never ate his vegetables? Would you stop providing food and shelter to your daughter if she didn't spend hours talking to you every single day? Of course not.

There's no holy measuring stick God keeps to track my prayer time. But if I forfeit this time, I'm the one who loses. When I do set aside time to pour my heart out or surrender an offense or a burden, I am the one who benefits. Just like my son who eats his vegetables or my daughter who gets to know me better. The benefits of prayer are a healthy spiritual life and the ability to know God and be known.

Prayer connects us in a supernatural intimacy to his Spirit. It opens the door to a gargantuan stack of colorful presents filled with his holy presence. Take your pick: love, joy, peace, patience, kindness, goodness, gentleness, self-control, mercy, forgiveness, understanding. Precious mean mom, what do you need today? It's there for the asking. It's up to you to take that gift and open it. Prayer helps you do just that.

> Or what man is there among you who, if his son asks for bread, will give him a stone? Or if he asks for a fish, will he give him a serpent? If you then, being evil, know how to give good gifts to your children, how much more will your Father who is in heaven give good things to those who ask Him! (Matt. 7:9–11 NKJV)

Wisdom

Mean moms understand that as our children grow, our role changes from a coach who tells them which position to take and calls out every play to a hands-off advisor. If we struggle with stepping into our advisor roles, we struggle with control. And control is just the code word for fear. Prayer reminds us we are not in control. God is.

> *Mean moms understand that as our children grow, our role changes from a coach who tells them which position to take and calls out every play to a hands-off advisor. If we struggle with stepping into our advisor roles, we struggle with control. And control is just the code word for fear. Prayer reminds us we are not in control. God is.*

Prayer falls into two main categories for me: asking for wisdom to make the wisest mean mom decision and intercessory prayer for my child.

I like to say, small children—small problems; big children—big problems. Motherhood comes with a million questions. When I'm experiencing another *What do I do now?* moment, prayer must happen. No matter what my kid's age, I need help, and praying for wisdom is a prayer God answers. He says so. "If any of you lacks wisdom, let him ask of God, who gives to all liberally and without reproach, and it will be given to him" (James 1:5 NKJV).

Walk

"I have no greater joy than to hear that my children walk in truth" (3 John 1:4 NKJV). So praying for this end result is my pleasure. If your son or daughter is not walking this way, keep the faith, mom. God loves your kids even more than you do. Pray without ceasing.

Fretting magnifies the problem, but prayer magnifies God. —JOANNA WEAVER

I polled my mean mom team about the importance of prayer in their lives and how they pray for their children. They had much to share with you. I couldn't have said it better.

> One thing that helps me stay consistent in prayer for my kids is to choose a verse each month that identifies something they are going through or need prayer for. I put their name into the verse and then write it on an index card. I keep the cards on my nightstand so I can read through them before I go to bed at night or in the morning. For that month, I pray that prayer. Then I choose a new one each month. For example: 2 Timothy 1:7—For God did not give Lisa (my daughter) a spirit of timidity. Remind her that in You she has power, love, and self-discipline. —LARA VAN HULZEN

I had a wise mom-friend whose favorite verse was Jeremiah 33:3: "Call to Me, and I will answer you, and show you great and mighty things, which you do not know" (NKJV). She called it God's phone number. —MITZI LIMBURG

I pray over my boys every morning and every evening. And during the day, when I think about it, I pray for them then, too. I've prayed with my youngest and he always thanked me. He knows how to pray himself now.

The oldest might be more of a "I'll believe in you, Lord, if you do (insert favor here) for me" kind of kid. Not sure where he stands right now as an adult; of course he tells his momma what she wants to hear. I believe that even if your kids don't pray themselves, it's still our responsibility to pray for them. My youngest and I do pray before our meal when we go out to a restaurant. I think kids learn when you lead. However, I'm almost 100 percent sure that he and his buddies don't pray when they go out for sushi. —KATIE CHANEY

Our bedtime consisted of family prayers, and then we all sang the song from the end of the Lawrence Welk Show: "Good night, sleep tight, and pleasant dreams to you. . . ." The kids enjoyed it as much as we did. We had them pray as much or as little as they wanted at bedtime. They outgrew the song eventually, but we've continued to pray with them (and for them) over the years. They learned through this process we are a praying family. Then, and even more so now. Now, at twenty-two, nineteen, and fifteen, they ask us to pray for them and with them. We consider it a privilege, and know it is something we can always do for them and usually the most effective!
—KIMBERLY FREEMAN

When my son was young, I prayed 1 John 2:24–25: "As for you, see that what you have heard from the beginning remains in you. If it does, you also will remain in the Son and in the Father. And this is what he promised us—eternal life." My prayer for my family this year is that they love the Lord their God with all their heart, soul, mind, and strength (Mark 12:30). I'm not perfect at this, but my heart is ever toward God's intervention in our lives. I want our family to be known as a family that makes Mark 12:30 evident. —MITZI LIMBURG

When my child thinks I'm mean because of a boundary I've laid down, when I'm struggling with something they've said or done, or when they're struggling with something I've said or done—prayer is my next step.

Prayer does not move Almighty God to respond the way I want him to. God is not a puppet, so we don't get to pull his strings. If that were the case, he wouldn't be God. Prayer changes me. It brings me to a place of surrender and peace, ultimately abiding in him. When I wholly lean on him, his words abide in me, and what I ask in his will, he promises he will do (John 15:7). Prayer pulls me in, closer to him. And when I draw near to him, he promises to draw near to me (James 4:8).

I have lived long enough to see God respond miraculously after heartfelt prayers from this mean mom's hurting heart. Prayer has been the salve that cooled the burns of many fiery trials of motherhood. Prayer has been my peace-giver, calming my nerves after two-year-old tantrums and teenage sass, and prayer has been the life preserver I have thrown in the direction of many a drowning mom-friend in need of supernatural rescue. Whether my children are six or sixty, as a mean mom, prayer is the most powerful tool I have.

Mom to Mom

What does prayer look like in your mean mom life?

⌒I used to pray for God to change my husband and my children. When I prayed for him to make me aware of where he wanted to change me, I started seeing answers

... answers that kept me so busy I didn't have any more time to nitpick anyone else. —CHERI GREGORY

I always tell people that nothing brings me to my knees faster than my kids. —LARA VAN HULZEN

We pray as a family, often stopping in our tracks to join in prayer when the need arises. We also share praises, which reminds all of us that God is working.

Nurturing a healthy prayer life works best when I remember my family is not me. We all have personal relationships with God. We all have different personalities. It's not my place to judge how they pray. It is, however, my privilege and responsibility to live as an example and let them see the power of prayer blooming in my life. —XOCHI E. DIXON

I've been a praying mom for over twenty-five years, but felt my prayers were sometimes ineffective. A few months ago, I asked God to teach me how to pray more effectively for my family. I figure if the disciples could ask, so could I. God placed me in a group of praying moms who taught me to use my sword of the Spirit. I'm now praying with more power and authority over my family. My husband and I pray specific Scriptures over our children and each other every morning. Our prayer time has caught fire! And we're seeing changes and growth in our family. —BETH THOMPSON

PART TWO

Mean Moms and Munchkins

CHAPTER SIX

Mean Moms Model Honor

- -

Seeds of respect sow humility and harvest honor.
—Joanne Kraft

My kids and I were watching a Disney sitcom recently. In the last scene, the seven-year-old character chased his brother through the house. Mom stops the tiny sprinter, puts her hand on her hip, and says, "What did I say about running in the house?"

To which her son replies with the same hand on his hip, "What did I say about talking back, woman?" The laugh track explodes with chuckles.

Except there's nothing funny about this.

To me, it's an example of a growing problem: lack of respect in children. It's been the rallying cry of every older generation, "Kids need to show a little respect." And it's true.

Some might say, "It's just a kid show. You're taking this fictional family too seriously." But I would beg to disagree: you might not be taking this problem seriously enough.

There are many influencers in our children's lives, and TV is just one of them. Since the 1950s, there have been thousands of studies done, and all but eighteen conclude watching violent shows is also linked to having less empathy toward others. *Extensive research indicates that media violence can contribute to aggressive behavior.*[1] The point I'm trying to make is, if my children can learn violent behavior and a lack of empathy by watching television shows, they can learn disrespect in the same way.

Our family laughs a lot together. Paul and I share a background in police work, which helps in just about any situation, no matter how dark. But there are a few things that aren't funny, and disrespect is one of them.

Mean moms can sniff out disrespectful behavior like a bluetick coonhound. Respect is an imperative character trait for future success. How my children treat me is a good indicator of how they'll treat their teachers, their future employers, and eventually their spouses. But respect is just the first step. What I desire most for them to learn is honor.

> *Mean moms can sniff out disrespectful behavior like a bluetick coonhound. Respect is an imperative character trait for future success. How my children treat me is how they'll treat their teachers, their future employers, and eventually their spouses.*

Honor Brings a Blessing

Respect is an outward action of deference and sometimes just a good learned habit. It is a lesson best taught in the classroom of your home. Respect is a mindset that travels to the heart and blossoms into honor. Think of it this way: respect focuses on outward behavior, doing or saying the courteous thing. Humility shows this respect to all. Respect and humility working together create honor and point to a person's worth or value; thus, outward courtesy to everyone not only becomes habit-forming but works its way into the heart.

"The fear of the LORD is the instruction of wisdom, and before honor is humility" (Prov. 15:33 NKJV). In this verse, the word *fear* means a holy respect. So, by God's own Word, respect is the first step and humility the second step before honor is rooted in each of us. Respect courteously acknowledges a person, while honor attaches worth to that person.

Honor is a godly virtue so important to God that he desires a child reflect this posture toward him and even toward parents. God sealed the deal in his Ten Commandments: "Honor your father and your mother, that your days may be long upon the land which the LORD your God is giving you" (Exod. 20:12 NKJV). It's the only commandment with a blessing tied to it—obedience with benefits.

This is how important honor is to God, and the first step to this glorious place is to teach respect. It's a fundamental lesson I instill in my children daily. Respect and humility are iron threads that keep relationships from unraveling.

Faith . . . teaches us not merely to tolerate one another but to respect one another—to show a regard for different views, and the courtesy to listen. —PRESIDENT GEORGE W. BUSH [2]

Make a point to communicate to your child how important respect is to people. Then share how people speak different languages, have different skin color, live in different places, do different things, but all are God's creation and valued by him. When we show others respect, we show God honor. Teach your child the following four Scripture verses:

- Honor all people. Love the brotherhood. Fear God. Honor the king. (1 Pet. 2:17 NKJV)
- A gracious woman retains honor. (Prov. 11:16a NKJV)
- Honor your father and mother, and, You shall love your neighbor as yourself. (Matt. 19:19 ESV)
- Do nothing out of selfish ambition or vain conceit. Rather, in humility value others above yourselves. (Phil. 2:3)

Home Training 101

When our family moved to Tennessee, I was surprised at the children here. I've been around children with manners, but this was amazing. While we were staying at a local hotel, we were able to interact with the other families each morning at breakfast time. When three local school basketball teams showed up, I was anticipating kids to be kids. After a few days of living around these young athletes, I made a few observations.

These children put my four to shame. Their manners and kindness were off the charts. They said excuse me if they happened to come in contact with adults in the crowded dining room. They asked, "Which floor, ma'am?" when we entered an elevator together, punching the number for me each time.

Weeks later, I attended Samuel's parent sports meeting at his public junior high school. This is where I was introduced to the southern old-school definition of raising kids with manners. The principal called it *home training*. She was kind but firm and made it clear she expected this behavior on and off the field if any of our children ended up making the cut.

"You parents are doing a great job," she said. "I expect your children to treat one another, their teachers, and myself with respect and kindness, and behave in a way that brings honor to our campus. My grandma is from Louisiana; she calls this kind of behavior *home training*. I believe many of you already are training your children this way."

When the meeting was over, dozens of wannabe football players stood in a single line to shake the hand of their principal and new football coach. My husband and I were impressed with the courtesy of these kids and the respect they showed.

Model Respect—Great Kids Are Watching

Great kids aren't born with great morals and stellar character traits. It takes a childhood of daily lessons by diligent parents and their supporting family and friends to reinforce these values. There's no magic pill we can give children to guarantee they become adults who are selfless, kind, or even respectful. But there are a few things mean moms do very well that make a difference in molding a great kid.

Model. Manners can't be taught. They must be caught. Teach your children by example. If our kids are going to learn, they have to learn by watching us first. Hold open doors. Offer to let someone go in front of you in line at the grocery store. Keep your thoughts to yourself while you're on the road. Shake hands and say thank you.

Expect. Expect good manners from great kids. They will rise to the level of your expectations. Mean moms don't tolerate disrespect, so they raise the bar with their expectations when it comes to respecting others.

Praise. Praise your children publicly, in front of their siblings or anyone else in earshot.

> *There's no magic pill we can give children to guarantee they become adults who are selfless, kind, or even respectful. But there are a few things mean moms do very well that make a difference in molding a great kid.*

Correct. Gently but firmly remind your kids not to dash to the front of the buffet line or interrupt when someone's talking. Never shame. Be consistent.

―――――――――――――――――――――――

I loved you enough not to make excuses for your lack of respect or your bad manners. —ERMA BOMBECK

―――――――――――――――――――――――

Samuel, our son, was seven years old when he discovered it was rude to yell "hey" to get the attention of a waitress. "Son, do you realize how disrespectful that is? What you should say instead is excuse me, or pardon me. See how much nicer that sounds?" Minutes later, Samuel suffered manners-amnesia and hailed our waitress once again with a loud "hey."

"Samuel, I want to explain something to you. This young woman is working harder tonight than you've worked all your life. It's hurtful and disrespectful to get her attention that way."

Home training lesson #4227 was now in session. I told him, "Okay, son, after you apologize to her for yelling at her, for the rest of the meal if you want to engage any of us in conversation, you need to precede with 'excuse me' or 'pardon me.'"

"Aw, Mom, really?"

"Yep."

The rest of that meal, Samuel had the opportunity to practice his new skill. We appreciated his formality—which included much dramatic flair. He hasn't suffered from manners-amnesia since. Be ready. Teachable moments come along when you least expect them.

Respect Begins with Manners

Before children read their first book from cover to cover, they begin with the primary lesson, sounding out the alphabet and learning their vowels. The same can be said about respect—it begins with lessons in good manners.

Modeling respectful behavior starts at the top and trickles down. Think about it. How do you speak to your parents—their grandparents? Do you make a point to hold open doors and give away your seat to strangers? Whatever you do they'll eventually do, too. Whatever you don't do, don't expect your child to do, either.

Repetition is the next step. We have a new Lab puppy who isn't potty trained. We take her out the same door over and over again. This week, she began walking to the door herself. Forgive me for the comparison, but dog training and teaching good manners to children are similar. Every day, I have the opportunity to teach my children respect. How I speak to my husband shows them how to speak to their brother or sister—over and over and over, until eventually they learn.

Modeling manners and daily repetition are the one-two punch to teach manners to your children.

Are you wondering where to begin? I've included a list of ten simple manners every great kid should know. It's a beginner's list, so there's nothing too difficult. I don't include anything about how to sit at the table or where to place a shrimp fork. Every great kid knows these basic ten, and as adults they'll never forget them. That's the beauty of manners. The benefits are timeless.

10 Simple Manners Every Great Kid Should Know
- *Please and thank you.* Those magic words learned as toddlers can't be overused. When my husband invited some young adults out to dinner with our family, it was disappointing when they didn't thank him for their meal. You know you're successful at teaching respect when your kids publicly express thankfulness, and you're not around to hear it.

- *Offer a seat.* Our family spent our summer vacation in New York City. It was quite an experience being around thousands of people all day long. When we rode the subway, I was thrilled to see Samuel stand up and give his seat to a woman who seemed surprised and very grateful for his generosity.
- *Hold the door.* We've taught our children to hold a door for strangers walking in or out of a building—an act of kindness that should be applied liberally and not be restricted by age, sex, or creed. Remember, humility respects everyone.
- *Clear the table.* Whether we're hosting company or we're invited to a friend's home for dinner, our children get up and clear the table. It's up to the hostess to halt their charitable act. Adults admire kids who serve, and children survive a ten-minute chore and thrive on the encouragement of a grateful hostess.
- *Treat her like a lady.* We live by this old-fashioned rule of thumb. When my boys become men who drop a woman at a front door first and then go park in the rain, or offer food to their wives before heaping dinner on their own plate, I will be thankful. There's a lot to be said for encouraging chivalry in our boys.
- *Carry in groceries or help with bags.* Manners can become helpful tools, especially when we get home from the grocery store. Our children don't just run into the house—they grab the bags and bring them into the kitchen first. When company comes over, the kids are the ones who assist with guests' coats and bags.
- *Use last names first.* This might look a little different depending on what part of the country you're from.

We introduce an adult to our children as *Mr.* or *Mrs. So-and-So*. It's up to the adults to correct us and offer their first names to our children. Now, here in the South, they have their own way. I've noticed children refer to my husband and me as Miss Joanne or Mr. Paul.

- *Technology gets a time-out.* When the grandparents visit or company is over, technology needs a time-out. There is nothing more disrespectful to a grandparent or anyone over the age of twenty-five, for that matter, than competing for the attention of a child with an opponent who jingles, chirps, lights up, and vibrates. Turn off technology and put it away until company leaves.
- *Say sir and ma'am.* Living in Tennessee, I hear *ma'am* and *sir* all the time. Our kids now do the same. It's pretty close to being a term of endearment around here. When a young man holds open the door and I thank him, he'll acknowledge me and say, "Ma'am." Good manners—there's nothing better.
- *Send thank you cards.* This is important. It's a lesson I learned later in life. Some might say, "Why should I send a thank you card if I've already thanked them in person?" Because it's the perfect respect exercise.

Mean Moms Model Patriotism

When Lee Greenwood's song "God Bless the USA" plays on the radio, my eyes well up with tears. Last night, I watched this American icon perform the song live alongside country legend Charlie Daniels and singer Luke Bryan at a benefit concert for veterans. Go ahead and check that one off my bucket list. Living in the South has its perks, and patriotism is one of them.

When I first moved to the South, I noticed a few things were a little different here. American flags fly year-round—lots of them. And when they celebrate America's birthday, you'd better duck and cover. These folks celebrate—explosively. *I about had a heart attack.*

As the child of a veteran, I was raised to respect those who serve our country. My parents modeled this lesson by the way they spoke to men and women in our armed forces. I watched my father walk up to men in uniform and heard him say so often, "Thank you for your service, son." Our children see it now in the way Paul and I model the same example. Just recently, a US Marine stood in line for lunch in his dress blues. Paul bought this young man's meal, and our children overheard their father's words: "Thank you for your service, son."

Lots of people say, "I respect our military." I'm sure they do. But our children are taught to honor them. We take them to veterans memorials and Civil War cemeteries, reminding them "freedom is not free"—a quote they saw this summer etched in stone in Washington, DC, at the Korean War Veterans Memorial. I believe respect puts up a flag on a national holiday. Honor sheds a tear when it flies.

I remind our children, "You and I are living here by no effort of our own, but by God's grace and the selfless service so many in our country have volunteered for—hundreds of thousands paying the ultimate sacrifice." My husband is a former police officer, so respect doesn't end with our military; it continues in how we treat our emergency service leaders who risk their lives every day, as well as public servants like teachers and ministry leaders. Respect is shown to all.

Great Kids Make Mistakes

Remember, great kids make mistakes, too. When my child is disrespectful, I respond appropriately. I don't embarrass or ridicule;

I'm firm but kind. Still, it's important to address each situation, sometimes publicly, and never to shame but lovingly correct.

When I was a little girl, there was a season when I walked home from grammar school followed by two schoolmates. These neighbor boys were friends who one day made lewd comments and gestures. When I shared with my mom what was happening, my father contacted the parents of each boy.

The next morning, I opened the door to find one of the young boys who'd been harassing me. He stood on my porch, looking a bit awkward, and apologized quickly, offered a handwritten apology, and was gone.

I never heard a word from the other boy.

The boy who apologized was a great kid raised by great parents who took advantage of a disappointing situation to teach their son respect. Today, the boy who left the note of apology, my former neighbor and current friend, is a retired veteran of the United States Army. He spent his life flying OH-58D Kiowa Warrior helicopters and has taught pilots for nineteen years. He recently reminded me that I started that argument thirty years ago, which I've conveniently forgotten. A veteran of the Gulf Wars, his career of choice was to serve the American people. He was taught the meaning of respect as a young boy and grew up to be a man of honor.

Humility Brings Honor

I've made a lot of mistakes as a mom. My children would be more than happy to sit you down and share a story or two *or twelve*. There's that time I was so frustrated I punted an enormous tin of popcorn across the family room, sending a shower of fluffy salted clouds raining down over their heads and onto the floor. Or that time I charged in to referee an argument and vented my frustration on the wrong child. Yeah, my list is long. I love what author Lysa TerKeurst says: "Bad moments don't make bad moms." I'd like to extend her quote to add, "Bad moments don't make bad moms. They open the door to a humble moment."

When I asked my mean mom friends how to teach a child respect, humility was at the top of the list:

> I believe the single most important key to earning my kids' respect has been walking in humility toward them. It's not usually the great things I've accomplished or done right that earn their respect, but the times I've quickly admitted where I'm wrong and where I fall short, especially with my teenagers. They see hypocrisy so clearly, and when they do, they lose all respect. My master's degree and published book, they think that's pretty cool. But, their mom on her knees before them and asking for their forgiveness as a sinner saved by Grace? That leaves a lasting mark. —Teasi Cannon

---

Asking forgiveness when I'm wrong goes a long way toward earning my child's respect. —LAURIE BATDORFF

Respect is *not* a one-way street. Expecting it only from my children is wrong. They must be the recipient of it first. I am not called to put my child in a place of honor, above me as a parent, but I should respect their opinions, value their words and their ideas, and give them both of my ears to listen when they want to share something with me.

If I see myself as "right" and knowing more all the time, or as having more important things to do than listen to their incessant ramblings, I have set myself high on a throne of pride. *The Message* translates Proverbs 16:18 this way: "First pride, then the crash—the bigger the ego, the harder the fall."

But, when I remember I was once a child, and sit beside them and show them they matter, or ask forgiveness for a mistake or a hurtful word I may have used—I teach my child humility.

Humility is one of the great marks of a crucified man. —ANDREW MURRAY

Jesus Christ is our perfect example of humility and honor. Our holy God stooped as low as supernaturally possible to our sin-sick level, sacrificing all for me and you. And because I believe this, I love him. Respect courteously acknowledges someone died for a cause—honor is to love this person because of it. There is no greater teacher of respect than a humble mom, and a humble mom is a glorious model of honor to her child. Let it be so with every mean mom.

Mom to Mom

How do you teach respect?

Certain manners were expected in school, and we incorporated them into our parenting. This includes teaching them to respect another adult, by using *Yes ma'am* and *Yes sir*, even when they don't want to. My husband and I are convinced we instill respect by not backing down from the values and beliefs we have.
—LAURIE HAYS

We teach our boys to open doors for people. I believe that is a part of respecting others. I know our culture isn't always interested in raising gentlemen who do things for women, but I still want my boys to be gentlemen.

—LINDSEY BELL

❧I gave my boys the freedom to be angry with me—they were never allowed to be disrespectful.

—KATIE CHANEY

❧We are a military family, so our kids have been taught the importance of the national anthem and how to behave when it's sung. They have a love for their country and understand what an important job and choice it is for our military to protect us . . . as all Americans should. We attend parades in the community whenever we can, and the kids love to show their pride and love for our servicemembers and their sacrifice. —KELLA PRICE

❧I believe the best way to teach a child respect is to respect them. How you talk to them and react to them, etc. Also, by modeling what respect looks like, especially when you interact with others, including your hubby. Respect to me is not yelling "What?" when they holler a question from another room in the house. Respect is using "Yes ma'am." And "Thank you." And not rolling the eyes when asked to do something. —JENNA MARTUCCI

Notes

[1] Kyla Boyse, "Television and Children," University of Michigan Health System website, www.med.umich.edu/yourchild/topics/tv.htm.

[2] George W. Bush, "Remarks at the National Prayer Breakfast" (speech, Hilton Hotel, Washington, DC, February 1, 2001), http://www.gpo.gov/fdsys /pkg/PPP-2001-book1/pdf/PPP-2001-book1-doc-pg42.pdf.

CHAPTER SEVEN

Mean Moms Don't Take Sides

If you want to stop an argument, shut your mouth.
—Charles R. Swindoll, *Hand Me Another Brick Bible Companion*

There's nothing that sends a mom to the moon faster than bickering kids. Could someone tell me why a moving vehicle is a favorite venue? Driving under the influence of toddlers and teenagers should be as illegal as alcohol or texting. Why, yes, I'd vote for this legislation. I've had too many near-fatal accidents where I silently willed my Chevy Suburban off a cliff.

"Mom! David just threw something at me."

"Knock it off, David. Don't throw things at your sister."

"But, Mom, Meghan threw her gum wrapper at me first!"

"I did not!"

"Liar! You did, too!"

What is it about me getting on the phone or behind the wheel of a car that makes my children lose their ever-loving minds? It's these magical moments of motherhood they never tell you about— the ones where children test boundaries and drag you along for the ride. If you've been mothering for a few years and have more than one child, you know exactly what I'm talking about. And if you don't, it's only a matter of time before you ask your husband, or your girlfriend, or your mailman this question: Why do my kids fight so much?

Why?

This million-dollar question rears its ugly head after visiting a friend whose children love each other so much they finish each other's sentences. Her children seem so happy together, like medicated-happy, and you just don't get it. You begin to ask yourself, *Why do (insert friend's name here)'s kids like each other? Why do her children share toys and talk to each other sweetly, while my two act like alley cats who want to rip each other's eyes out? What am I doing wrong?*

First, don't be fooled. I am sure your friend's kids fight, too. Children argue and fight for all sorts of reasons. It's been going on since the beginning of time. The Bible gives us lots of examples of the friction between siblings: Leah and Rachel, Jacob and Esau, and before you think your kids are the worst at getting along, let's not forget about Cain and Abel. I'm sure Adam and Eve had a lot of the same concerns. Siblings have been bickering since creation. Remember, nothing is new under the sun. It might help to identify the triggers that could spark World War III.

Competition. Each child wants mom and dad's full attention. It's not a shock. Children want as much love and affection—and did I say attention?—as you can give, and then some more. If another little somebody comes on the scene, they'll soon be stepping on enemy territory. Remember, their mommy and daddy's hearts belong to them. The fight is on, and they'll show their parents that whatever their sibling can do, they can do better.

Possessiveness. All tiny little tots start here. Their things become an extension of themselves. They want their toy, their chair, their stuffed animal, and if you even touch it, you're going to hear about it. I promise. As they get older, they will grow out of this—you hope so, anyway. Teenagers are similar. Just try going into their room and borrowing something without asking—God be with the sibling who disregards a teenager's boundary.

Control. As sibling dynamics go, most of the time, the older child is the bossiest. He or she uses this technique as a way to control younger sibs. The child is making a statement: "This is my world. You're just living in it." Control is fear-based. This child is afraid of losing first place—competitive for mommy and daddy's love. See *Competition.*

Fairness. This is one is huge. It begins young. I said "Not fair!" to my mom when I bought my first car, a white 1976 Ford Elite with red interior, while my younger sister was *given* a light blue Volkswagen Bug. "Not fair!" (I'm not bitter or anything.)

It's important to train a child to understand that unfairness happens—a lot. When they shout these words, there will be times you'll have to agree with them. Mean moms know this is a huge character builder.

Our older two children were raised when we didn't have the discretionary income we have with our youngest two. Needless to say, our big vacation was a road trip in a leaky minivan and staying in what my adult son, David, calls "hooker hotels." Our youngest son, Samuel, is about to embark on a seven-day Caribbean cruise. Fair? Not on your life. If that four-letter word is used in our home, my husband enjoys reminding the culprit, "I'll know you're concerned about fairness when you're as upset about something unfair in your favor."

"You're right. Things aren't always fair." We remind our children often, "Life isn't fair"—not to make them feel bad but to

Mean moms don't make everything fair in their homes. If you do, you set your child up for failure as an adult.

prepare them for adulthood. They will experience this even more the older they get, and we can't control life's outcomes for them. Let your child feel this. Mean moms don't make everything *fair* in their homes. If you do, you set your child up for failure as an adult. Fairness is an illusion. It doesn't exist. As author Steve Arterburn says, "Fair is where pigs go to win ribbons."

Parenting Evolution

Charles Darwin's *The Origin of Species* was published in November 1859. It was the world's introduction to his theory of evolution. But Noah Webster defined the word *evolution* more than thirty years *earlier* this way: "Evolution: A series of things unrolled or unfolded; as the evolution of ages."

I am a believer in Noah Webster's earlier definition. Motherhood evolves. Parenting skills evolve. A mom learns to adapt to each of her child's needs to motivate and guide. Parenting is a series of experiences that unroll and unfold over the ages. Each event in the past quarter of a century of my mom journey has affected the parent I am today. Following are a few lessons I use now with bickering kids.

Don't referee. Allow your children a little time to try to settle their problem. Rushing in to judge one winner and one loser will only make the children resentful and make you very tired. Plus, when you don't referee, it empowers a child to learn how to work out a problem to resolution. That's a great lesson many of us adults still need to learn.

Don't encourage tattling. Never tell your child to spy on their sibling or another child. This is a selfish mom move. It puts a heavy burden on your child, while breaking down a sibling relationship in the process.

Don't compare. "This child shares. This child doesn't. This child is great at math. This child isn't." I often share that I have four children—two head kids and two heart kids. My head kids sift thoughts and decisions through logic first, while my two heart kids sift these same decisions through emotions and feelings first.

What has this done? It caused my head kids to think they didn't have as big a heart as their heart-first siblings. This wasn't my intention. Convincing a child what you believe about them almost always starts with words. "Don't compare your children, Joey." This was my mom's last bit of parenting wisdom before she passed away. I bring her words back to mind so often.

Preparation Is Key

Margo dreaded bringing her kids to the grocery store. She broke out in a cold sweat before she stepped foot beyond the sliding glass doors. Like a switch had been turned on, immediately her two began taunting each other and poking at each other, whining and complaining. After only five minutes, she was frazzled and on her last teeny nerve.

Can you relate? I sure can. How do you keep from pulling over your grocery cart in the middle of the bread aisle to swing 'em like a dead cat? Don't judge me. You know you've wanted to. Losing your cool never helps. Screaming their names like they've scored the winning touchdown at the Super Bowl means you've lost control. You don't want to do that, either. When you yell, you lose. Game over.

How do you curb the frustration? I believe the answer always lies in the preparation. You may think it's crazy to *prepare* for bickering kids, but it's saved the lives of my four children countless times. When you ready yourself for a skirmish, you won't be ambushed by surprise attacks that make you white-hot angry. When you have a plan, you don't react when your mind is a scrambled mess of furious. You respond instead.

React: An emotional response to anger or fear. All mammals have reactive DNA. Conflict drives an emotional answer, and words or actions aren't thought through.

Respond: A reasoned answer based on cognitive, level-headed perception to understand and strategize the next deliberate act on our part. Our reply remains in a place of integrity and is consistent with our values and beliefs.

A Lesson in Response Preparation

Grace and Samuel walked into the room with their heads hung low. They had something to tell me. Earlier, while arguing over who should replace the toilet paper in their bathroom, they busted their vanity door. Apparently, their argument blossomed into a Van Halen after party—except they aren't rock stars. Did I mention this was in our brand-spanking-new house?

Cue the scary music . . .

After taking a few minutes alone in my bedroom to regroup, breathe deeply, and pray I didn't kill them (*prepare*), I calmly told them to get me a piece of paper. As they sat quietly on the couch, I proceeded to write a list of chores that would keep them busy for a long, long time (*respond*). I was prepared, and I responded. No yelling at all. Here's a tip about preparation. It benefits you, too.

⟋

Won't stop fighting? *Vacuum the rugs.*

Can't stop tormenting your sister? *Clean the baseboards with a toothbrush.*

Continue to take your brother's things without asking? *Make his bed for the week.*

Arguing over a TV show? *TV is off for two days. Read a book instead. Better yet, read that book to your little brother.*

⟋

Home Remedies

There's a popular Pinterest photo of two siblings in an extra-large, white T-shirt. They look like a miserable two-headed monster with words in black permanent marker on the front: *Our Get-Along Shirt.* I laughed when I saw it. As much as it probably pained two sisters to be in such close proximity after a skirmish, it brought me back to when I was a young mom with two bickering children.

"Mom! David touched my book. I told him to leave it where it was and he knocked it off the table . . . *on purpose!*"

"No, I didn't. I *accidentally* brushed alongside it and it fell. *She* is the one who kicked my backpack down the hallway first!"

On and on this went.

"Okay, you two, come here." This is when I did the unthinkable. "Meghan, hug your brother."

"No way!"

"Yes way. Hug him. Now you, son. Hug your sister."

"Gross."

"Yep, I agree. Hearing you two argue and fight is pretty gross. Now hug each other."

A hug happened like a flash of lightning—that fast. Before they retreated, I told them, "Now, Meghan, tell your brother three reasons why you love him and make sure to use his name each time you do."

I remember hearing once that the sweetest sound to a person is his or her own name. Don't know if it's true, but I figured it didn't hurt to add that to their consequence. This is when my daughter would give an Olympic-sized eye roll and sigh in great anguish. "David, I love you because . . . you're funny."

"Look in his eyes when you tell him, Meghan."

"Aw, Mom, seriously?" *Eye roll. Shrug. Deep sigh.*

"David, I love you because you're good at catching bugs and animals. David, I love you because you love me."

"Okay, I'm not sure that last one should count, but I'll let it slide. Son, it's your turn. Tell your sister three reasons why you love her."

"Can't you just spank me instead?"

"Nope."

As fast as he could, he blurted, "Meghan, Iloveyoubecauseyou're-nicefunnyandloveme."

"Okay, okay, um, yeah, about that, that's not going to count. David, look in your sister's eyes and tell her three reasons you love her. You can't just repeat what she said. Rules, ya know."

"Mom, this is horrible," he whined. But in the next sweet moment, he looked up at his big sister and softly said, "Meghan, I love you because you read stories to me. Meghan, I love you because you make up fun games to play. *Geesh, this stinks,*" he mumbled. "Meghan, I love you because you share your chocolate milk with me sometimes."

Now, I can't tell you if this helped cement their adult friendship today, but it's a memory they recall fondly. Some might say forcing a child to communicate something they don't want to say is wrong. I believe encouraging them to focus on how they truly feel about each other for a few minutes is beneficial.

When our children grow up, they will have lots more opportunities to bicker and argue—it's called marriage. If by some tiny chance they've learned to see past an offense to remember the truth about the person who hurt them, then it's worth it. "For the moment, all discipline seems painful rather than pleasant, but later it yields the peaceful fruit of righteousness to those who have been trained by it" (Heb. 12:11 ESV).

Will You Forgive Me?

Forgiveness. How do you teach this to a child? Instead of training our children to say, "I'm sorry," we've taught to them to ask forgiveness. Saying I'm sorry is reserved for harm without intent, like dropping a glass of milk or accidentally stepping on a toy and breaking it. Sorrow is subjective.

Forgiveness is objective. There's no middle ground. It's either offered or it's not. You're either forgiven or you're not. "Will you forgive me?" Forgiveness is a motive of the heart. Anyone can apologize without remorse—just follow politics for a while. I love what Aaron Earls has to say on his blog *The Wardrobe Door* about teaching forgiveness after an offense or sin.

Why My Kids Don't Say I'm Sorry

The real Gospel tells us there is nothing that can make our sin acceptable. . . . We do not apologize for our sin; we confess it as sin and trust in Christ's finished work on the cross to justify us before God.

When someone has sinned against us and we respond with "That's OK," we do so in direct contradiction to what God has said. It is not OK. Sin is never OK. It can and should be forgiven, but it should be recognized first as sin and treated as such.

After our two boys get in an argument, as they so often do . . . we make them ask, "Will you forgive me?" and respond, "I forgive you." When I sin against my boys or my wife, I'm supposed to ask for forgiveness and they, in turn, should respond with forgiveness.

That better represents the Gospel we are trying to reinforce in our family. If we continually repeat phrases that belittle the severity of sin, we unintentionally construct a false gospel in the hearts of our children. Sin is seen as something of little, if any, consequence, which requires little, if any, repentance.

Words matter, and because they do, I want to continually affirm the true Gospel, not a counterfeit version, in the lives of my two children. . . . [I] reinforce the truth to my sons that sin matters more than we like to admit, but forgiveness is available more than we dare to dream.[1]

Bickering children are a mean mom's best opportunity to teach forgiveness. God gives us so many reminders of what forgiveness looks like in the Bible. Here are a couple of verses every great kid should know.

Forgive us our debts, as we also have forgiven our debtors. (Matt. 6:12)

Then Peter came to Jesus and asked, "Lord, how many times shall I forgive my brother or sister who sins against me? Up to seven times?" Jesus answered, "I tell you, not seven times, but seventy-seven times." (Matt. 18:21–22)

I can look back over my forty-six years and see many tender places where forgiveness was generously given and received. Areas remain where it's still needed. I fail often with peripheral relationships in my life—friends, extended family. Holy work in progress. But, as a woman of faith, I'm determined for my children to see it modeled.

Forgiveness in action is the only way it's taught. The world's greatest example? Christ on the cross. How can I hold a grudge when he has done so much for me? Why do I hesitate to pursue debt's release when God paved the way with his only Son's blood? When I put my eyes on Calvary, any offense I've suffered melts away.

A Beautiful Benefit

Want to know a beautiful benefit to the reconciliation of siblings? They no longer see each other as an enemy. That title now belongs to you. Why? Because you're the mean mom who gave them a chore or took away something they loved like their iPod or iPhone, or turned off their favorite TV show, or gave them a time-out, or taught them about forgiveness. Which is great, because now those same two kids who were trying to gouge each other's eyes out magically become allies, like Franklin D. Roosevelt and Winston Churchill, right before your eyes.

The next time your little angels are acting like drunken sailors on payday, just imagine me whispering in your ear this golden nugget of truth: don't be afraid of bickering kids. Nothing brings them closer than serving time together.

Mom to Mom

How do you handle bickering kids?

The boys were fighting, so I called them into my room: "Do you know what I'm going to say?" I asked them. "Yes," said my ten-year-old. "It's the same conversation we always have." He looked at his brother and said, "Let's just get this over with and hug each other." —JENNY LUNDQUIST

I have three boys (six, four, and two) and when the bickering gets out of hand, I make them run laps or I give them a chore to do. Clean the toilet seat with a baby wipe, get clothes out of the dryer, clean handprints off the window, bring me daddy's dirty clothes, bring in firewood—nothing too mean or dangerous. —JEN BUNDY

When my kids bicker and argue, I take away the privilege of talking to each other. —STEPHANIE MORRIS

Discipline when they bicker varies based on the child. What works for one doesn't necessarily work for the other, so we try to have natural consequences. If they fight over a toy, the toy goes in time-out. We encourage them to work out problems on their own. I step in when I think it's needed, but I don't want to be a referee for their whole childhood. —ERIKA HRANICKY

I'm very fortunate my two boys rarely bicker. There was this one time they wouldn't stop, so I told them to sit on the couch and hold hands until they could get along again. They laughed so much the argument was quickly forgotten. —KAREN MARSHALL

When my children fight over a toy or something tangible, it becomes mine. Over time they learned to work it out because if they didn't, nobody got to play with it. —ANN GOADE

When our kids bicker, we make them say two to three nice things about each other. So far this has worked. Most of the time they end up doubled over in laughter. There's a few moments it was a stretch to find something to say to each other, but they did it. It has helped cut the thick air of bickering. —RACHEL TEMPLE

Notes

[1] Aaron Earls, "Why My Kids Don't Say 'I'm Sorry,'" *The Wardrobe Door* (blog), July 11, 2013, http://thewardrobedoor.com/2013/07/why-my-kids-dont-say-im-sorry.html. Used with permission.

CHAPTER EIGHT

Mean Moms Make 'em Work

God honors work, so honor God in your work.
—Max Lucado

A re your children at an age where they can go to the potty by themselves? Then there's no reason your little darlings can't help you around the house.

Martha Stewart might not be impressed with my shower, nor would she praise me for my windows, but my home is in good enough shape for company. I learned early on that with four children, I have four helpers to get work done around the house. My children call it slave labor; I call it a benevolent dictatorship.

When friends complain their houses are a mess, yet they have able-bodied kids at home, I just don't understand it. Children may not be able to clean a dish like you can, but remember, if they can understand their PS3 and iPhone, they're capable of maneuvering a mop and a dust rag. Many of you reading these words are exhausted. You look like you've been run over by a truck, with toys strewn around every room like plastic land mines, and last week's dishes fermenting in the sink. Time to put on your mean mom pants and see things clearly—you're not helping your kids or yourself.

Each morning, your children roll out of bed and make their breakfast, get dressed (throwing their pj's on the floor or, if you're lucky, in the dirty-clothes basket where magical fairies clean, fold, and put them away each week), and head off to school. When they get home, they do homework, watch TV or play video games, get shuttled to an activity or two, gobble dinner (leaving the plates on the table for you to clear), and then head to bed and start all over again in the morning.

This is marshmallow mom insanity. The definition of insanity is doing the same thing over and over but expecting a different result. Nothing will change until you take the lead and teach your kids a different way. So, here are a few tips and tools to help you get some of your sanity back and mold your children into responsible, capable, independent adults.

Create a chore chart. If you're the analytical, linear type, this is right up your alley. After twenty years of parenting, I've tried the weekly chore list, the monthly chore list, and so on. We now give a child a responsibility for a year or two. I was sick of the fighting and the complaining if one child wasn't home to do the dishes. So once Meghan moved out, David had dishes for a few years. When David moved on to mowing the lawn and daily garbage, Grace took his place at the sink. Samuel is next in line for kitchen detail, but while he waits, he clears and sets the table each night. If one of the kids isn't home to do his or her chore, another child picks up the slack, which reinforces the "it's not fair" lesson. It works for us.

Assign daily responsibilities. Every morning, our kids make their beds, clear out the dishwasher, dump the garbage, make their breakfast, and put their dishes in the dishwasher. If you've never asked your little ones to play a part in this type of house-work, you're in for a challenge. Hold tight and hang on; stand your ground. As they come to understand they are a part of a family and see you're not backing down, they will learn to accept their new responsibilities. Most importantly, come alongside them. When you work together, they may grumble, but they'll feel included.

Make it fun. Housecleaning doesn't have to be drudgery. Put on a song and tell the kids they have until it's over to finish one of their chores. Dance around when you vacuum. Kids follow our cues. If we're annoyed, they'll be annoyed. If we're joyful, it's contagious. A mom sets the thermostat in her home when it comes to a good or bad attitude.

> God will reward even the meanest drudgery done from a sense of duty, and with a view to glorify Him. —MATTHEW HENRY[1]

Servant of All

There's a holy by-product to teaching children chores and responsibility—servanthood. The central theme of the Bible is Jesus Christ—God put on flesh. The King of kings came not to be served but to serve.

> For even the Son of Man did not come to be served, but to serve, and to give His life a ransom for many. (Mark 10:45 NKJV)

> [Christ Jesus], being in the form of God, did not consider it robbery to be equal with God, but made Himself of no reputation, taking the form of a bondservant, and coming in the likeness of men. (Phil. 2:6–7 NKJV)

Tucked inside the Gospel of John is the story of the Last Supper. The night before Christ's crucifixion is a supernatural model for serving.

> And supper being ended, the devil having already put
> it into the heart of Judas Iscariot, Simon's son, to betray
> Him, Jesus, knowing that the Father had given all things
> into His hands, and that He had come from God and
> was going to God, rose from supper and laid aside His
> garments, took a towel and girded Himself. After that,
> He poured water into a basin and began to wash the
> disciples' feet, and to wipe them with the towel with
> which He was girded. (John 13:2–5 NKJV)

Washing feet was the ultimate dirty job of Jesus' day. The poor didn't own shoes. Sandals were the common footwear if you had the money, so you can imagine what a shepherd's foot looked like after walking behind sheep all day. The sole of the sandal was a piece of cowhide cut in the shape of the foot. Since walking was the most common mode of transportation, feet were filthy.

Still, Jesus washed the feet of his disciples—each and every one—then explained the reason for it.

> He said to them, "Do you know what I have done to you?
> You call Me Teacher and Lord, and you say well, for so I
> am. If I then, your Lord and Teacher, have washed your
> feet, you also ought to wash one another's feet. For I have
> given you an example, that you should do as I have done
> to you. (John 13:12–15 NKJV)

When your children complain about chores, or serving, share the story of Jesus. Discover together the only One who left Heaven and humbled himself to death for us. There's no greater example of loving service. It's sacrificial servanthood at its finest. If I want to raise an adult who is selfless while serving, I must point to Jesus.

Do you want to teach your child leadership? Teach him how to serve. Do you want him to be a respected adult? Teach him there's no job beneath him. Reverend Martin Luther King, Jr., said, "Life's most persistent and urgent question is, what are you doing for others?"[2] He was echoing the Apostle Paul's words to the Philippians centuries before: "Let each of you look out not only for his own interests, but also for the interests of others" (Phil. 2:4 NKJV).

Chores Earn Respect

Eric, my brother-in-law, remembering when he was a youngster, said, "My neighborhood friends would gather at our house on Saturday mornings. My mom would make them all breakfast, and before we could take off and ride our bikes or play ball at the park, my dad had chores for us to do. He barked them out to all my friends: sweep floors, clean up the garage, take garbage out. Whatever he needed done, we did it. We didn't question it. It's just how it was. There was no money exchanged. When my father passed away, each of those boys were men who came and paid their respects to my dad. They loved him."

Do you want to teach your child leadership? Teach him how to serve. Do you want him to be a respected adult? Teach him there's no job beneath him.

Our two adult children love to remind us, "You and Dad are not the same parents. You've gotten really soft! We had to do a lot more chores than these two have." David points at his younger siblings. Within seconds, he and Meghan gang up on us and the game begins: Who can share the worst chore-war stories?

"Remember when Mom dumped out all my dresser drawers and made me sort my clothes and fold everything back up again?"

"I don't know what Grace is complaining about. When I had to clean the kitchen, there were six of us. She's got it made."

When I talk with parents, it seems we have a common desire— to raise our children to become independent, responsible, hard-working, God-honoring adults. So why do we steal opportunities to grow them into this kind of person?

Remember marshmallow mom Maria Myhiolcantdothat? She steals teaching moments from her children daily. Each time we make an excuse and do something our kids can do, we rob our children of one more lesson of hard work and responsibility.

How else will they learn to be independent if we don't add responsibilities to their shoulders?

Do you want your child to be a hardworking adult? If so, then stop using these excuses when it comes to chores:

"They're too young to pick up their toys."

"They should be having fun. They've got their whole lives for have-tos and to-dos."

"I pick up their bedroom and make their bed. It only takes me five minutes."

"It's easier if I vacuum. They don't do it right. They go around the furniture, and I like to move the furniture."

"Washing the dishes and putting them away might mean they break something."

"Wash their own clothes—are you kidding?"

Kids will rise to the level of your expectations. Expect them to be lazy or lackluster in their duties, and that's what you'll get—every time.

Mean Moms Don't Rescue Their Child

When we moved to our rental home in Spring Hill, Tennessee, we were on an acre of green grass. All our neighbors had riding mowers. When I say all, I really mean all, ya'll. The country songs you hear about people mowing "big grass"—that's not a myth. Grass grows supernaturally fast, which means lawns need to be mowed *a lot*.

Our family never lived on acreage before. So we checked Craigslist and bought ourselves a gas-powered push mower. We divided the acre into thirds and gave each of our three still-living-at-home kids their new responsibility. They were not very happy.

When we first showed Samuel his new chore, I asked him what he thought. He smirked, "I think God is testing me. He's testing my endurance. He's testing my patience."

His older sister shared, "I hated it with a passion. It's cruel and unusual punishment. Which is, by the way, a violation of the Eighth Amendment of the United States Constitution."

I followed up by asking Samuel, "Do your friends mow their own lawns?"

"No, their parents have other people mow their lawns because their parents love them."

I know this is how my kids will earn their bragging rights. This is an investment, a small lesson to form them into the adult people I want them to be.

But My Kids Won't Do Chores

Maybe your children are still whining and complaining about helping. It takes time and much encouragement to establish the habit.

Hang in there. Turn the tables on them and do what we did. Our children can be a little competitive at times. We tell them to out-nice each other. Beat that other person at being kind. Surprise them and make their bed. Clear the dishwasher out or pick up their toys for them. My kids get along so much better when their sibling lends them a hand.

"Teach your children first things first. Once chores are done, then you can play. Doing work together teaches a team effort. Working hard shows them life isn't all about them and not to be self-centered. It shows them what they start they finish. Hard work can bring a family close."

—SHARON HATCHER

"How do you get your kids to do their chores? Mine just won't do them." This question boggles my mind. I've received it more than I care to admit. I like to return this question with a question of my own: "When they come home from school, do they watch TV or play video games?" Chores become a habit for the kids when they've become a habit for us moms first. In the beginning, you may have to walk around with them each day until their responsibilities are complete.

If we don't stay consistent, or follow up by checking their work to encourage them every day, what we're telling them is, *It doesn't really matter if you do your chores or not.* And we miss out on an opportunity to give accolades for a job well done.

In our home, TV isn't on until chores are done. There's grace given for a job forgotten, but if they have a bad habit of daily-chore-amnesia, then it's time to pull the plug on electronics or whatever else they enjoy for a while. Mean moms are consistent. Completed daily chores means free time for them. Incomplete daily chores means consequences. Which usually means more chores.

"My friend gets paid five dollars to clean the kitchen," Samuel complained. "I wonder what it must be like to get money for hard labor," he moaned as he collected garbage from the bathroom.

Don't expect to be their favorite person if you take away a privilege or two. Cleaning toilets and sorting the laundry is not on their grateful list. But you will earn quite a few mean mom blue ribbons of achievement when you instill chores that teach them hard work and responsibility.

Labor is God's education. —RALPH WALDO EMERSON[3]

The Strictest Mom in the World

The World's Strictest Parents is a reality show on the CMT channel. Wayward kids are placed in a home with loving boundaries for a week. For seven days, kids are taught what seems foreign to them—hard work, responsibility, and respect—while the world watches an amazing transformation take place. These wild and rebellious kids are tamed and learn to understand their value. What's even more miraculous is that the parents who host these kids, the parents they originally hated when they arrived, are the ones they hug and weep over when they have to return to their own homes.

I spoke with Sharon Hatcher, one of the "strict" parents highlighted on this reality show. I must admit, after watching her family's episode, they didn't seem all that strict to me. Sharon's family owns a dairy farm in Middle Tennessee. I asked her what she wanted her legacy to be as a parent. She shared that the biggest lesson a mean mom can teach her kids is a good work ethic. "Teach your children first things first. Once chores are done, then you can play. Doing work together teaches a team effort. Working hard shows them life isn't all about them and not to be self-centered.

It shows them what they start they finish. Hard work can bring a family close."

She went on to tell me, "After our episode aired, I can't tell you how many calls we received from people all over the country begging us to take their kids and teach them about hard work and responsibility."

Sharon Hatcher is a new grandma today with two successful grown-up kids, who both understand the value of hard work. I'm not sure I've known a family that works harder than they do. She wears her *mean mom* title proudly, and her kids are now adults who love her for it.

Don't Miss an Opportunity

Mean Moms don't waste an opportunity to teach children about servanthood.

Years ago, I remember being at a church potluck event. After the meal concluded, it was the men and women who jumped up to clear tables, scrape dishes, collect garbage, and wash utensils, while the kids went off to play. Where were the teenagers? Why wasn't the youth group elected to help at this event? Where were the kids, period?

Call me old school, but I'm not sure I'll ever understand why some churches don't enlist their youth group for events. Mean Moms don't waste an opportunity to teach children about servanthood. I guarantee your child will never wake up and tell you, "I can't wait to help someone today for no money and zero recognition!"

The next time you're at a family gathering, a friend's house, or even at your own kitchen table, remind your children Jesus is our perfect example. He says so himself. "I have set you an example that you should do as I have done for you" (John 13:15). Then gently remind them to get up and bless others with a little selfless serving.

It's not mean to ask your children to lend you a hand each day, even if you have time to do it yourself. If they don't follow through, it's not mean to tell them they can't play with their friends, watch TV, play on their iPad or their Xbox, or do anything else they want to do. It's not mean at all.

Mom to Mom

What do mean moms think about hard work?

❧ A mean mom is someone who requires much from her children in the way of respect, discipline, hard work, and a servant's heart. Mean moms are not here to be their kids' *BFF*, but rather to love, teach, and nurture their children into becoming God-fearing, secure, productive adults. —SHEA CORSETTI

❧ Having boys, food is a huge motivator. I have a little verse posted on our pantry: "The one who is unwilling to work shall not eat" (2 Thess. 3:10). —KELLA PRICE

❧ I tell my kids, "Inch by inch, anything's a cinch!" —TEASI CANNON

❧ If there's one thing I wish I could go back and redo, it's how I talked to my kids. I'd ban the words *bright* and *gifted* and focus on the value of *hard work* and persistence. —CHERI GREGORY

❧ "Get up and get it done—then celebrate with time for fun!" If my kids had a quarter for every time they heard me say that, they'd be independently wealthy.

—DANICA HUIZAR

If my kids complain something is too hard, like, you know . . . putting their shoes away, I tell them, "You were made to do hard things." —ASHLEY GERHARD

Notes

[1] Matthew Henry, *Matthew Henry's Concise Commentary on the Whole Bible* (Nashville: Thomas Nelson, 1997).

[2] Ryan Scott, "Best Gift for Martin Luther King Jr.'s Birthday? Social Impact," *Forbes*, January 17, 2013, www.forbes.com/sites/causeintegration/2013/01/17/best-gift-for-martin-luther-king-jr-s-birthday-social-impact.

[3] Ralph Waldo Emerson, *The Complete Works of Ralph Waldo Emerson,* First Series (Memphis: General Books, 2009).

CHAPTER NINE

Mean Moms Use Their Words

To encourage someone is to inspire them to have courage.
—**Patrick Morley**

Words matter. They hold the power to encourage or discourage, to give wings to our children's dreams or destroy them. The Bible tells us death and life are in the power of the tongue (Prov. 18:21). We will be held accountable one day for careless words spoken (Matt. 12:36). You might not want to stand in line behind me when my accountability session happens. Still, that's how important our words are.

When my children were little, I remember pouring positive words into them . . . thinking I had this encouragement thing down. My words would make them soar. I just knew it.

"Meghan, you brought home straight As! You are amazing!"

"David, you are gifted, son. No one is a natural with animals like you are."

Here's something I've learned. There's a difference between encouragement and praise. Let's use intelligence as our example. The above words I used with my children are praise, and they have the opposite effect of encouraging a child. Why? Because I set them up for failure, and while I believe failure is a valuable experience, I don't want to be the reason they have more of it. Praising a smart son or daughter for his or her intelligence may make the youngster anxious and ill-equipped to deal with failure, a team of psychologists has found. "It is much better to praise a child for effort," said Claudia Mueller and Carol Dweck, researchers at Columbia University.[1]

It's fascinating how parents, me included, put intelligence high on the list of crowning achievements. For the same reason we shouldn't put our daughter's outward beauty in a continual spotlight, or our son's gift of athletics, we should refrain from doing it with intelligence. Mean moms understand hard work. Effort. Dedication. Perseverance. A heart that makes kind, humble, and sacrificial choices should be where we shine a spotlight.

> *Mean moms understand hard work. Effort. Dedication. Perseverance. A heart that makes kind, humble, and sacrificial choices should be where we shine a spotlight.*

Melody Mychildisgifted is a marshmallow mom. She puts her daughter high up on a pedestal. Thanks to Melody, her daughter believes her smarts make her as unique as a snowflake. Instead of feeling special, her child is trained to believe parental love is wrapped up in good grades. So when she brings home her first C, she's devastated. Melody's conditional affection keeps her daughter from sharing her deepest longing—to be loved for who she is, not for what she does.

"Praising children's intelligence, far from boosting their self-esteem, encourages them to embrace self-defeating behaviors such as worrying about failure and avoiding risks," said Dr. Dweck. "However, when children are taught the value of concentrating, strategizing and working hard when dealing with academic challenges, this *encourages* them to sustain their motivation, performance and self-esteem."[2]

Jesus Was Encouraged

God knows how important encouragement is to his kids. We see a beautiful picture of encouragement in the Gospel of Matthew. When Jesus is baptized, his cousin John assists this holy dunking and is witness to this miraculous moment as our Lord breaches the water. "And a voice from heaven said, 'This is my Son, whom I love; with him I am well pleased'" (Matt. 3:17). God models how parents should encourage their children.

Identification. God tells the world, "This is my Son." Jesus can identify with belonging to a loving father. There is value in knowing your family claims you as theirs. Belonging is so very important, especially when it's not results-oriented or work-based. Love with no strings attached.

Unconditional love. This was the very beginning of Jesus' ministry. His most incredible work was yet to be done. Still, God lets everyone know his Son is loved. This is vital to encouraging children. They must know they are loved for the mere fact they are yours. I tell my children, "There's nothing you can do to make me love you more." Your child needs to know that.

Public praise. God has this one down when he tells the world about his Son: "With him I am well pleased." Do you publicly admit to being well pleased with your children? When was the last time you let the world know how grateful you are to be your child's mom?

Dalton

My husband is an attorney. From time to time, I tag along with him when he has to be in court. Recently, he was appointed to represent a mother who was trying to regain custody of her teenage son,

Dalton. After some poor decisions by his mother, this young boy was now in the care of foster parents.

I watched as this child walked in and sat down outside the court room, dressed all in black. He listened to music on his iPod with earbuds, drowning out the world. His body language screamed, "Leave me alone and stay away." His whole demeanor saddened me. Every mommy-fiber in me wanted to give him a hug.

I watched as his social worker sat down beside him. Dalton took out his earbuds as she put her arm around his shoulder and began talking with him. "I just finished reading your reports. I am so proud of you. You are doing so much better in school. Your hard work is paying off! You are my shining star," she said, while smiling from ear to ear.

It was like watching a deflated balloon fill up with air. With each word of encouragement, this young man's whole countenance changed. The once wilted flower began to stand tall after a long and much-needed drink. I wanted to cry for him. God's Word says, "The tongue has the power of life and death," and it's true. I witnessed life being poured into this child right before my eyes.

Encouragement Is Not Praise

When I dug into my Bible, I discovered the word for praise, *yadah* (יָדָה *yä·dä'*), means to confess to, to laud, or be thankful to, as in, "Let everything that has breath *praise* the LORD" (Ps. 150:6).

Now, I'll be the first to admit I'm thankful *for* my kids—but I'm definitely not thankful *to* them. But when I say things like, "You give my life meaning. You are my purpose. If it weren't for you, I would be lost," I'm praising them.

As sweet and innocent as those words sound, it's not only praise-worthy lingo, but it puts a lot of pressure on your kids. A friend and I were chatting about decisions we made as teenagers and a few our own kids have made. She likes to tell parents, "One day your kids will surprise you." And she doesn't mean in a good way. So if you've praised your children and they make a mistake or let you down, they have a pretty rough fall.

Dr. Kevin Leman says, "Encouraging instead of praising is tricky business." He goes on to explain it this way: "Praise says, You're great *because* you did something. Encouragement says, It's great *something was done* and I *appreciate* it."[3]

Giving encouragement isn't simply a matter of praising what children do. Every parent must be aware of the very fine line here. Many people—adults and children—believe that unless I perform, achieve, or do something, I won't be approved or loved. The key to encouraging children is their own perception of what you're saying. When they do something right, good, or productive you want to focus on what they did.

Encouraging words focus on the act, while praise puts all eyes on the person. —JOANNE KRAFT

The Hebrew word for encourage, *chazaq* (חָזַק *khä•zak'*), means to strengthen, to restore, to grow firm, and to give courage. It shows up four times in the Bible, and two of those times are within the first three chapters of the Book of Joshua. "But charge Joshua, and *encourage* him, and strengthen him: for he shall go over before this people, and he shall cause them to inherit the land which thou shalt see" (Deut. 3:28 KJV, emphasis mine).

After forty years, Joshua was about to lead the Hebrew people into the Promised Land. Moses was Joshua's spiritual father and was given the important task of encouraging him for the work ahead. Moses never tells Joshua, "You are so much better than anyone else here." Or, "We couldn't do this without you." Nope. Moses tells him to be strong and courageous and reminds him,

"The Lord is with you wherever you go." He encouraged Joshua to trust God along the way.

I learned this *encourage instead of praise* lesson much later in my parenting journey. Now, when my little ones surprise me with cleaning the kitchen, or bringing home a good grade, I'll say, "You worked really hard cleaning up in there. I really appreciate all your help." Or, "Congratulations on seeing your hard work pay off. It must feel good to bring home an A." I take my focus off the children and place it on their effort instead. It reminds them they can do it—not because they're smarter than anyone else or better than anyone else, but because they will put in the effort to succeed. And, whether they do it perfectly or not, I love them.

Everyday Encouragement

You couldn't pay me to step back in time to attend school again. I still cringe when I come across my fourth grade picture: pimples, crooked teeth, and a pixie haircut I never wanted. School years can be tough for any growing child. I'm not sure Grace will ever forget her first day of preschool and the fears that necessitated a quick wardrobe change. Now that she's a teenager, she doesn't much appreciate her siblings' memories being so clear about that event.

I haven't met anyone who comes out on the other side of their school years without a few bumps and bruises. The summer of 2012, our cross-country move was exceptionally difficult for me as a mom—Grace and Samuel were experiencing their first day of school in a new state. Not just any school—junior high. And, to make things even more difficult, the culture was a little different and the language was a little different, which meant our kids would look and sound even different.

How do I encourage my children when they're worried about making friends? How do I instill hope in a child who is having trouble sleeping because she's worried about fitting in? I've included a few ways our family worked on breathing courage into our little ones during this time.

Open God's Word. It's the first place to start, always. For the Word of God is alive and powerful. It is sharper than the sharpest two-edged sword, cutting between soul and spirit, between joint and marrow. It exposes our innermost thoughts and desires (Heb. 4:12 NKJV).

When we began our trek across the country to the new state we'd call home, our morning devotion was reading the book of Joshua, verse by verse and chapter by chapter. Instill courage in your child by sharing the words of Joshua, "Be strong and courageous. Do not be afraid . . . for the LORD your God will be with you wherever you go" (Josh. 1:9). We reminded our kids they were embarking on a new promised land. It would be an adventure, and God would be with them through it all.

Read a story. Barbara Rainey, co-founder of Family Life Ministries, has written some wonderful read-aloud story books for children. The first week of school, we read the book *Growing Together in Courage*. The story we read on the eve of their very first day of school was about a young girl named Sophie Scholl who grew up during World War II and stood up against Hitler's movement. Would you believe the highlighted verse was Joshua 1:9? The same verse that began our family's cross-country journey together.

Pray together. Prayer is powerful. Can you imagine what peace it brings our children to hear us pray for them and with them? Most parents tuck their children in at night, so take an extra minute and pray out loud so they hear your petitions before a good and gracious God. When I pray with my sons, I thank God for making them mighty men of valor like Gideon in the Bible. The more common our prayer time with them becomes, the more open the children will be to joining in. There's nothing sweeter than hearing your child pray.

When the alarm went off on their first day of school, my stomach did a quick flop. There's nothing that touches the lives of my four children that doesn't touch me, too. God feels the same way about each one of us. So take a moment and encourage your kids. You're breathing courage into their lives and teaching them to lean on God in the process.

Encouragement Breeds Encouragement

Blue Oak Elementary School in Cameron Park, California, began a program called How Full Is Your Bucket?—based on the children's book of the same title written by Tom Rath and Mary Reckmeyer.[4]

The story tells the tale of a young boy named Felix who has an invisible bucket hanging over his head. Every time Felix performs or receives a negative action, his bucket dips down and water is released. The reverse occurs every time Felix does something positive. By the end of the story, readers are left with the message that each action affects others either for good or for bad. Readers are encouraged to perform actions that fill up their bucket rather than empty it.

Teacher Michael Bird saw this lesson first used with his own children at their grammar school and began implementing it in his own classroom. Bird initiated this program by having his students write notes called *drops*, which are appropriately named because they are written on pieces of paper in the shape of water droplets.

Once the drops are completed, students place them in a bucket in the classroom. On these drops, the children write a note that encourages a classmate or recognizes a positive action by another student. These actions include befriending a peer who feels left out, picking up a piece of trash around the school, or taking someone to the nurse when he or she feels sick—the list goes on and on.[5]

This idea was an incredible boost to students when our children attended the school. Principal Paul Stewart grabbed the baton from his colleague, teacher Michael Bird, and introduced it to the rest of the classrooms at Blue Oak Elementary. It's been highly successful.

What a beautiful example of growing our kids with encouragement. Encouragement is life to our children. The examples around us are astounding. If God makes a point to show all of us how he feels about his Son, we need to do the same with ours.

Mom to Mom

What does encouragement look like in your home?

e ⁓I try to encourage my kids by talking with them, not just talking at them. I don't want to just pass out accolades. I want to affirm and engage in conversation to (1) make sure they understand the depth of my pleasure and love for them, and (2) get feedback on how they feel about themselves. —JESSICA WOLSTENHOLM

e ⁓We told our kids that they were bright and gifted, under the guise of wanting them to maximize their potential. What we were really doing was basing our value as parents on our kids' performances and, unbeknownst to us, setting them up to fail. —CHERI GREGORY

e ⁓Encourage kids and leave a note in their lunch box or on their pillow. —SAUNDRIA KECK

e ⁓Prayer, short sticky notes, hugs, and words of affirmation encourage my boys. I try to focus on their strengths to build them up. —MICHELE BUSCHINI

e ⁓We try to praise their effort more than the outcomes, e.g., rather than make a big deal about test scores, we

---

praise the effort they put into studying. We hope to help them develop overall characteristics of persistence and self-discipline, when we remind them it's not their performance that matters, but their participation.

—ADELLE GABRIELSON

℮ If my kids struggle with not feeling confident about something, I remind them to tap into how they felt when they aced a math test or were kickin' booty on the soccer field. Then I'll remind them, regardless of the outcome, that all anyone can do is their best. Learn what you can from the experience, accept it as character building, and get excited about the next level! —DANICA HUIZAR

Notes

[1] "Praise Children for Effort, Not Intelligence, Study Says," *New York Times*, web archives, July 14, 1998, www.nytimes.com/1998/07/14/science/praise-children-for-effort-not-intelligence-study-says.html.

[2] Ibid.

[3] Kevin Leman, *Bringing Up Kids without Tearing Them Down* (New York, NY: Delacorte Press, 1993).

[4] Tom Rath, Mary Reckmeyer, and Maurie Manning, *How Full Is Your Bucket?: For Kids* (New York: Gallup Press, 2009).

[5] Jessica Pratt, "Students Fill Buckets with Kindness," *Mountain Democrat* (Placerville, CA), December 28, 2011.

CHAPTER TEN

Mean Moms Say *No* to TV

- -

Most people buy the highest quality television sets,
only to watch the lowest quality television shows.
—Jarod Kintz

Want to be a mean mom? Turn off the TV. According to statistics, children in the United States spend nine hundred hours in school each year while spending fifteen hundred hours in front of the TV. When children between the ages of four and six years old were asked to choose between spending time with their father or with the television, 54 percent chose their flat screen. The saddest statistic to me is that 67 percent of American families eat in front of their television. Round it off, and that's seven out of every ten families who share their evening meal with NBC and Nickelodeon.[1]

TV has shoved aside our kitchen table to become the closest dinner companion to families today. Anyone else find this heartbreaking? Mean moms sure do.

TV has shoved aside our kitchen table to become the closest dinner companion to families today. Anyone else find this heart-breaking? Mean moms sure do.

Permit me to introduce you to a marshmallow mom who is near and dear to my heart: Lottie LetsthekidswatchTValot. Lottie is like most moms—but much worse. She began using colorful, musical DVDs to keep her toddler occupied while she picked up a little around the house or made a quick phone call. No harm, no foul, right?

Now that her kids are older, this tiny slice of screen time has warped into a full-fledged babysitter. It seems to her that her kids would rather watch their favorite cartoons than spend time with the family—and she's right. Dinner is the worst. In order to have a meal around the kitchen table, she must engage in hand-to-hand combat with her twelve-year-old for the remote. Defeated, she buys each child a television for their own room. Her justification? With the kids in their own bedrooms, finally she'll have some peace and quiet in the house.

TV Obstructs Communication

How well do you communicate with your child? Your biggest hurdle for a little face-to-face interaction may be the television.

Investigating solid research for this chapter began to depress me. Are you beginning to despise your high-definition flat-screen as much as I do yet? I've begun to change my thinking. TV is no friend of mine. It's a thief that steals precious time in my home with my permission. How often have I handed over the reins of my day to sit numbly and watch people I'll never meet act out their lives instead of living out my own?

When was the last time you turned off every television set and tuned in to your child instead?

According to the A.C. Nielsen Co., the average American watches more than four hours of TV each day (or 28 hours/week, or two months of nonstop TV-watching per year). In a 65-year life, that person will have spent nine years glued to the tube.[2]

As far as sweet marshmallow mom Lottie goes, it's a heart-wrenching shame. The flat screen with a thousand channels is her greatest child-raising nemesis, and she doesn't even know it. She opens the door wide to this sinister foe of her mom-child relationship and puts a TV in each bedroom, allowing whatever the cable networks deem worthy to keep her children's attention.

When was the last time you turned off every television set and tuned in to your child instead?

Meals Together Matter

During the Clinton administration, peace talks took place between Israeli Prime Minister Rabin and Palestinian dictator Arafat. As the press wildly snapped photos, the world witnessed a proud President Clinton standing behind the two world leaders as they shook hands.

Our pastor, familiar with the Middle East and deep traditions of the Jewish nation, wasn't as excited about the smiles and the warm grasp of hands. He told my husband, "You will know there is peace when they sit down and break bread together."

The breaking of bread is an expression of relationship and intimacy in many countries. And, if you stop and think about it, coming together for food and fellowship is an incredible opportunity to get to know one another in a much deeper way. According to every statistic I found, American families neglect this powerful time together. Dinnertime is one of the greatest opportunities to reconnect with your family every day.

Relationships are built and maintained upon communication. —CINDI MCMENAMIN

The Miraculous Kitchen Table

Miracles of the heart, supernatural comfort, and untold encouragement accurately define one tangible thing for me—our kitchen table. Do you understand the miraculous power of yours? If you're eating in your family room alongside *Dancing with the Stars*, you may not. Before I share some mean mom wisdom about meals, I need to share the sweetest gathering spot in my home.

Our kitchen table is made of wood, with a light pine stain. It's rectangular in shape with two drawers on one side. As with the pockets of a little boy's blue jeans, I open these drawers with trepidation. Half-eaten pieces of candy, Star Wars accessories, stray LEGOs, and plastic Barbie shoes litter this small space.

This table has sentimental value for me. It's where Grace held her nose with one small hand and her fork with the other—shoving broccoli in under the watchful eyes of her daddy. It's the place in our home where arguments have erupted between me and my teenagers. Where siblings have shared bowls of ice cream, and where I've knowingly squeezed Paul's leg under the table, gently reminding him to show grace with the kids.

Birthday cakes have been served, Christmas buffets eaten, and Thanksgiving feasts enjoyed. I've wept and prayed with friends over tea, laughed over misshapen homework disasters, and grieved the loss of loved ones. Devotions with my children have taken place here, and thousands of bowls of cereal have been poured.

My father-in-law built this table with his own hands. Just another reason it's so dear to me. Let me ask you this: How do you feel about your kitchen table? Here are a few ways to fall in love with yours again:

- *Give little ones a special job.* Grab a few pieces of paper to create personalized place mats for each member of the family. If your children are not lovers of the arts, allow them to place forks or napkins at each place setting. Send them out to grab some leaves to place on the table in the fall, or take a walk and pick wildflowers in the spring for a dinner bouquet.
- *Conduct cooking classes.* Bring your son or daughter into your stomping ground and let him or her chop, sauté, or stir right alongside you.
- *Invite someone new to share a meal.* Missionaries and world travelers have sat around our table; they shared stories of life in Russia, Australia, Mexico, China, and many more places, bringing the reality of godly adventures that much closer to our kids.
- *Hand your teen a twenty.* Her mission? To create a meal on a budget. Two things might happen: you'll be amazed by her gift of thriftiness, or you'll enjoy a hysterical meal of lemonade and Doritos.

Pull the Plug—We Did

Our family pulled the plug on cable TV for six years. I really thought I'd die without the Food Network, and how would I survive without putting my kids in front of a screen to free up my day? When we plugged it back in, we realized we weren't missing a thing. We put parental controls in place and kept the remote out of the kids' reach. Now we watch TV as a family when football is on or to watch a movie on Netflix. Once the game or movie is over, it's off.

I understand how our friend Lottie LetsthekidswatchTValot uses the TV to babysit every once in a while. *Dora the Explorer* is the best babysitter ever, *in my humble opinion*. But here's where the slope gets slippery. It was only a matter of time before I was battling a television show to sit down for a family meal. "Mom, can you just wait fifteen minutes? Our show is almost over."

And let's not overlook that time I watched the Super Bowl, and Janet Jackson had her "wardrobe malfunction"—um, yeah, thanks for that, Ms. Jackson. I loved sharing your intimate misfortune with my children in the room.

If there were background music set to my childhood years, it would be the theme song to the *Brady Bunch*. Sadly, these kinds of programs are tough to find. Apparently, our appetite for entertainment now includes naked first dates or watching incredibly wealthy people make warped life decisions and then attempt to survive them and convince us ridiculous is normal.

Americans turn screen stars into idols that steal our time. Does it really matter who Kim Kardashian is marrying? Or divorcing? One of our teenagers once shared, "It's Angelina Jolie's birthday today." To which I replied, "Hmm, I wonder if she'll remember your birthday this year." Try throwing in a little logic when you watch a show. You might come to the frustrating conclusion I did years ago: "We're watching yet another sitcom where the children are the smart ones and the parents are idiots."

As a Christian, I've often wondered: Would I be okay if Jesus were sitting beside me to watch my favorite program? Either I believe in Emmanuel (God with us) or I don't. I've been called to live a holy life set apart. Yes, there is abundant grace, but the change in me began when I started asking myself, *What am I modeling* for my children? Does this show reflect my spiritual lineage when I watch what I watch?

> But you are A CHOSEN RACE, A royal PRIESTHOOD, A
> HOLY NATION, A PEOPLE FOR God's OWN POSSESSION,
> so that you may proclaim the excellencies of Him who
> has called you out of darkness into His marvelous light.
> (1 Pet. 2:9 NASB)

According to a Gallup study, 77 percent of Americans identify themselves as Christian.[3] Is America truly a Christian nation? I'm not sure I believe that anymore. If this were really the case, there would be much less foolishness streamed into our homes. When a television show lacks an audience, it dies a swift death.

Be Diligent—Watchful

"Mom, can I go on Netflix and watch a movie while you're gone?" Samuel was calling me on my cell phone to ask. At the time, he was just shy of eleven years old, and pretty responsible.

"No, son, wait until I get home. I'll put a movie on for you."

I was driving Grace to youth group and could see her sigh and shrug in frustration at my response to her little brother. When I got off the phone, I asked her, "What? Why did you sigh like that?"

"Why can't he just put on a movie? I don't understand you sometimes. Samuel isn't going to put on anything he's not supposed to watch."

"Honey, I trust Samuel."

"Then why didn't you let him go on Netflix?"

"Grace, you kids are my responsibility. You know, honey, there's a Scripture that comes to mind: 'The enemy prowls around like a lion, to and fro, looking for someone to devour.' Think about it, a lion is going to look for the defenseless first. Your brother is home alone. I am not going to leave him defenseless. Your dad and I have gone on Netflix before and seen quite a few things we don't find very God-honoring—even with our website protections on. Why would I want your little brother to see some of those things?"

We'd arrived at church and Grace went off to meet her youth group leaders and practice for worship, while I met with my women's Bible study group. About fifteen minutes later, I could hear my daughter singing.

Being a proud mama, I just had to leave the study and walk toward the sanctuary for a better listen. Not wanting to embarrass her, I stood behind a door in the hallway, my eyes closed, listening to her melody. I silently thanked God for her desire to sing and prayed the words she sang so beautifully would sink deep into her heart. The band stopped midsong and started talking.

My daughter began to animate our earlier conversation in her junior high way: "Guys, listen to this, my mom won't even let me or my brother go on Netflix unless she's home with us. Can you believe it? She even started reciting Scripture." She used her best mom voice: "The enemy is like a lion, searching to and fro who he can devour."

As she talked about me, I stepped from behind the door and stood there, smiling. The kids in the band saw me first and said in unison, "Busted."

Grace looked shocked. Nervously she laughed, ran off the stage and across the sanctuary floor, and threw her arms around me, laughing while she said, "Mom! Were you there the whole time?"

"I sure was." I smiled down at her, not returning her hug. "And I have to admit, I'm really impressed. . . ."

"Mom, I'm sorry!" She continued to giggle nervously.

"I am proud of you."

"Proud of me?" She squeaked.

"You did a great job of reciting Scripture to your friends." I kissed her on the forehead and left. As a mean mom, it's not always fun making tough decisions, especially when my kids don't understand. As kids become preteens and then teenagers, there are daily opportunities to be labeled *mean*. I try to make the most of them and am occasionally surprised to discover they listen.

Be sober, be vigilant; because your adversary the devil walks about like a roaring lion, seeking whom he may devour. (1 PET. 5:8 NKJV)

What Are You Rooting For?

How do you know if a TV show is God-honoring or not? Most often, it's very clear. But for those grey areas, here's a good guide. Ask yourself: What am I rooting for?

Over the years, I've been sucked into a program or two. Lately, there haven't been many that I watched through to their last season. Why? Because I begin to root for sin. Let me give you an example.

Episode one: The first episode opens on an adorable family. Except, as the season continues, I'm convinced the wife is treated poorly by her husband. He forgets her birthday. He's a workaholic who's never home for dinner. Sure, he seems nice enough, but it's obvious he doesn't take time for her or the kids.

Episode four: The UPS guy comes by each day to drop off mail and talks to this poor, kind, attention-starved wife. He treats her nicely. In time, the UPS guy becomes a friend. He remembers her birthday and begins to share his thirty-minute lunch break with her. My heart responds to his tenderness toward her. *Sigh, isn't the UPS guy the best?*

Episode seven: It's official. I can't stand her uncaring, workaholic husband. I begin to think, *When is she going to leave this selfish lump and get together with the UPS guy?* Here's the defining moment. When I find myself rooting for an affair, I'm rooting for sin. That's when I know it's time to turn it off.

> I appeal to you therefore, brothers and sisters, by the mercies of God, to present your bodies as a living sacrifice, holy and acceptable to God, which is your spiritual worship. (Rom. 12:1 NRSV)

Here are a few helpful dos and don'ts for TV time together:

- Do set a time limit. It's amazing how fast the hours fly by when you're mesmerized by the TV.
- Do remind your children why you've chosen to watch a specific show together: great message, good example of family life, inspirational. Here's where you can practice dialogue and face-to-face communication.
- Do watch TV *with* your children. The moment I leave my children unsupervised, I willingly hand over my parenting responsibility to a network. These people market to make a buck and don't give a hoot about my kids or yours.
- Do the radical thing—turn it off. Pick up a deck of cards or play an old-fashioned game of charades. Sound ridiculous or silly? It may seem awkward at first, but I promise you'll laugh—a lot.
- Don't put a TV in your child's room—ever. Seriously. Never. Ever. You warp their creativity and encourage inactivity. Not to mention you welcome violence, profanity, and sexual content right into their bedroom. Please, mom, don't do it.
- Don't give a child an open invitation. TV is a privilege in our home—not a right. Our kids ask before turning it on: "Mom, I'm done with my homework. Do you

mind if I watch a show until dinner?" Then I ask the follow-up question: "What do you want to watch?" That way we communicate together about what gets center stage in our family room.

- Don't worry about what other people say. There will be some who think you're nuts. That's okay. When they witness your close relationship with your child, you can tell them why. TV was never meant to be a way of life. It wasn't created to be a member of the family. It is a slice of entertainment. Period. Don't give it more power than that.

We pulled the plug on cable television for six years. When we began our hiatus, I didn't believe I'd make it through a week, let alone seven years. We have TV now with limits. I rely on the truth that God hand-picked Paul and me to raise two daughters and two sons into adulthood. I'm not about to allow a flat-screen TV to steal away dinner time around our table or another moment that could strengthen our communication as a family. As a mean mom, I don't want to battle white noise for the attention of my sons and daughters, which is why I draw a deep line in the sand our television will never cross.

Mom to Mom

How does a mean mom navigate TV?

⌒We turn off the TV for dinner. Watching TV during a meal was not something I was raised with. Occasionally, we share a family room picnic and a movie, but otherwise it is off for meal time. —JENNA SCHMERSAHL MARTUCCI

Sadly, TV tended to be a built-in babysitter when the boys were younger. Being a single mom, in order to get things done around the house, I'd allow them to watch cartoons for hours! Then I started watching these *new* cartoons and I was terribly appalled. But the damage was done—you know how you can't *undo* something watched. I was careful from then on to monitor what they were viewing and limit their time in front of the tube. —KATIE CHANEY

Our kids earn their screen time (TV/video games) by doing extra chores around the house, above and beyond their normal duties or chores. They earn fifteen minutes of screen time per job by doing things like polishing the stainless appliances, folding a load of laundry, pulling weeds, etc. —ADELLE GABRIELSON

No TV in our home until all the chores and schoolwork are finished. If they get in trouble, no TV for a few days. We do occasionally eat lunch in front of the TV. But mostly because mommy just needs some quiet time. —JENNIFER PIERCE

Notes

[1] BLS American Time Use Survey, A. C. Nielson Co., quoted in "Television Watching Statistics," *Statistic Brain*, December 7, 2013, www.statisticbrain.com /television-watching-statistics.

[2] "Generation M2: Media in the Lives of 8- to 18-Year-Olds," The Henry J. Kaiser Family Foundation website, January 20, 2010, http://kff.org/other/event /generation-m2-media-in-the-lives-of.

[3] Frank Newport, "In U.S., 77% Identify as Christian," Gallup website, December 24, 2012, www.gallup.com/poll/159548/identify-christian.aspx.

PART THREE

Mean Moms
and Minivans

CHAPTER ELEVEN

Mean Moms Slay Goliath

I would rather be a little nobody, than be an evil somebody.
—Anonymous

ullies have been around for centuries. Who hasn't heard of the infamous nine-foot bully Goliath, David's nemesis? Preying on the weak, a bully uses lies, intimidation, and sometimes brute force to torment and shame his adversary. No one likes a bully. Maybe that's why I don't know anyone who named their kid Goliath.

Recently, a former acquaintance from high school attempted to friend me on Facebook. Seeing her photo and her name transported me back thirty years, when friends were my world and an angry pimple could derail my day. This gal was in the photography class at school. She thought it would be funny to come into the girl's locker room and practice her talent by snapping a few photos of an unsuspecting victim.

That victim was me.

When a black-and-white photo of me in my white Playtex bra circulated the "Jock Block" where the cool kids hung out and ate lunch, I willed myself to die. I'm a middle-aged woman, and my stomach still lurches when I think back on that day. I never shared this story with my parents. I was too ashamed and embarrassed. Plus, I was intimidated by this pint-sized bully.

Needless to say, I couldn't bring myself to accept her Facebook friendship. Seriously? What was she thinking? It made me wonder if I'd forgiven her or not. Is it forgiveness when you still fantasize about punching someone in the face? I believe I have, but what she did still hurts and conjures up shameful feelings. So whether I'm fourteen or forty, I won't befriend. I know I'm not the same person I was thirty years ago, and I imagine she isn't, either.

Actress Sandra Bullock has a good memory when it comes to her experiences of being bullied. "Kids are mean, and the sad thing is that I can still remember the first and last names of every one of those kids who were mean to me!"[1] It makes me wonder: Do the wounds of a bully leave scars forever? It was one thing to have this experience—quite another to be the mom of a child hurt in this way. I would've much rather been the victim.

When Your Child Is the Victim

Janene's daughter was thrilled to begin junior high. Nothing brought her more joy than growing up as quickly as possible. Though she craved adulthood, she had no desire to wear lots of makeup or change her long blonde hair. When Taylor came to her mom crying one day, Janene realized she hadn't been checking up on her daughter as regularly as she should have been—you know, having face-to-face time to really listen.

"What happened, Taylor?" Her mom stroked her hair as she cried into her pillow. After quite a bit of coaxing and even more comforting, her story came spilling out.

"When I went to school today, Ashley came over to me with her friends. She had a bag full of clothes and makeup. She knew I wanted to be Sandra Dee in the play *Grease*, and I told her I didn't want to put on eyeliner, and I didn't want to change my hair." She sniffled into a Kleenex. "Ashley got really frustrated with me. She told me, 'You know what I told my mom today, Taylor? I told her I was going to school to make an ugly girl pretty.'"

How does a bully find a victim? He or she begins with lies. "You're stupid. You're fat. You're ugly." Bullies speak lies into our children's identity. Mean moms understand words like these are used to hurt and can leave emotional scars into adulthood.

When you begin to believe untruths about yourself, it's that much harder to remember who your identity is in Christ. We need to pour into our kids God's truths that they are loved, accepted, and treasured, so they know lies when they hear them.

I am God's child. (John 1:12)
I am loved for all eternity. (Jer. 31:3)
I am surrounded by God's love. (Ps. 32:10)
I have direct access to God. (Eph. 2:18)
I'm redeemed and forgiven. (Col. 1:14)
I am complete in Christ. (Col. 2:10)

When you're a young girl, hearing someone publicly announce you're ugly is a lie that penetrates even the strongest of the strong. A bully wants your child to believe she is worthless. When the victim begins to believe falsely, the damage can last for years and years.

Bully Warning Signs

Unfortunately, junior high isn't the only magical age for bullying. Our son Samuel had his own run-in when he was in third grade. I was in the principal's office as soon as we knew, and thankfully with adult intervention it ended abruptly. I've learned the hard way that bullies are not just fictional characters on the big screen. They're real. And now with the Internet, there's even more opportunity for them to wreak havoc in your child's life.

With the age of technology, parents are doing their best to stay one step ahead of Instagram, Twitter, and texting. Who would have thought years ago there would be such a thing as cyberbullying? A *cyberbully* uses technology to harass, threaten, embarrass, or target another person by way of a social network post, photo, tweet, or text.

The FBI defines cyberbullying as willful and repeated harm inflicted through the use of computers, cell phones, and other electronic devices. Cyberbullying has become a growing concern. It includes sending threatening texts, posting or distributing libelous or harassing messages, and uploading or distributing hateful or humiliating images or videos to harm someone else. The article goes on to estimate that the number of children victimized ranges from 5 to 72 percent.[2] It's probably safe to say your child has been a victim or knows someone who has.

> *A cyberbully uses technology to harass, threaten, embarrass, or target another person by way of a social network post, photo, tweet, or text.*

According to a study published by Consumer Reports: "7.5 million under the age of thirteen are on Facebook."[3] Did you get that? Millions under the age of thirteen. Unbelievable. I cannot even fathom that. But more disturbing is that, under thirteen, you aren't eligible to have an account with Facebook in the first place. Which tells me one of two things: either the children signed up for accounts without their parents' permission, or their parents were aware and allowed them to.

As a bona fide mean mom, I choose to protect my child from this type of cyberbullying in the best way I know how. I say "no" to some technology— including smartphones. —JOANNE KRAFT

I've heard parents give lots of reasons for social media: "It's how kids communicate today." "Our family lives far away. They connect on Facebook." All good reasons, but unless you're sitting by your child's side 24/7, once they're unsupervised on the Internet, the door has just been flung wide open for a cyberbully or worse. No longer does a child need to be face-to-face to be victimized. Remember that.

Habits Mean Moms Use to Deflect Cyberbullies

Following are three things that help you spot any kind of bully in your child's life.

Look. Observe your children. Pay attention. Have there been changes in their behavior? Are they becoming withdrawn? Are they spending more time secluded in their bedroom with a laptop computer or iPad? Is there a change in their confidence level? A victim of a bully struggles with feeling ashamed. Avoiding people and painful situations becomes habitual.

Listen. Pay attention to what your children are telling you. If your children are very young, you might notice they're playing more aggressively with their stuffed animals, or their artwork is no longer filled with unicorns and rainbows. Older kids need to know you're there for them. Remind them you are willing to listen to anything they have to say. Then make a point not to lecture or monopolize the conversation. Give them the space they need to share.

Love. Remind your children how much you love them. Don't forget to encourage. Your love is the salve they need for their hurting hearts. It's embarrassing for children to admit being bullied. They feel helpless and insignificant. If your child is young, cuddle and hug him more. Teenagers act like they dislike the extra hugs, but don't be discouraged; they may be in big bodies, but they still love a hug from mom.

Mean Moms Know Their Worth and Teach Kids Their Value

Do you have a child who's being bullied? Maybe your child is the one doing the bullying. Do you want to make your children bully-free? Teach them their worth and value. From the time my kids were very young, I would say prayers with them at night, and then while sitting on the edge of the bed, I'd kiss and cuddle them. Rarely have I left their rooms without reminding them, "God has an incredible plan for your life. I can't wait to see what you accomplish together."

> *Do you want to make your children bully-free? Teach them their worth and value.*

There is no magic potion that will keep your children from being humiliated and hurt by other children. But when they know how much they mean to God and to you, it makes them a much tougher target for a bully to strike. Speak life-giving words into your child daily, such as, "I'm proud of you. I love you—no matter what."

Working at a police department is sometimes like having a front-row seat to a very sad movie. When I run a rap sheet and see the criminal history of a subject, it pains me. I can't help but think,

What happened to these men and women when they were young? Were they bullied or were they the bully? When was the moment they began to believe lies about themselves? I tell my children "hurt people hurt people." And hurting people don't know their worth.

How Much Are You Worth?[4]

As we walked inside the dollar store, our children ran off in different directions. My husband, Paul, followed me as I made a beeline to the gift wrap aisle where our children found us and were buzzing around once again. Our youngest was quiet. At eight years old, Samuel normally was a handful of busy. "Samuel, you're awful quiet today, son. Is everything okay?"

"How much does a foster kid cost?"

"How much does what cost?"

"How much does a foster kid cost?" he repeated. "My new friend Justin is a foster kid. He doesn't have a family. Do we have enough money to buy him?"

Words caught in my throat. Thankfully, my husband was quick to respond. "I'm not sure if we do, son. Have you even thought this through, Samuel? If you had someone living with us your age, you would have to share your room."

"I don't care about that, Dad. I feel bad he doesn't have a family."

Finding my voice, I asked, "So, how much do you think your friend costs?"

"He doesn't know, Mom. He thinks he's free, but he's going to ask his foster family tonight. He's going to meet me tomorrow at recess and tell me how much he's worth."

Samuel's words tore my heart in two. *He's going to meet me tomorrow at recess and tell me how much he's worth.*

That was all it took. On came the waterworks. My husband distracted our son while I stepped away to search for a tissue in my purse. I couldn't wrap my head around the fact that my son's new friend was trying to figure out what he was worth. As a foster child, his loss highlighted the value of family. His greatest desire was to belong to someone who would love him. So much so, for the sake of being loved, he was willing to hand his life over to the lowest bidder.

Many things come into play to make someone question his own value. But it didn't stop the questions from pressing heavy and hard. *Why doesn't this child know what he's worth? How can a child not understand his value?* When children struggle with their worth, they grow up to be adults who struggle with this same issue—their own self-worth. The loss of a marriage, the loss of a job or a home—these are all things we believe define our value in this world. Nothing could be more wrong.

Do you realize how precious you are to the Lord? Would you like to use some supernatural bully spray to keep your child from harm? Teach him these truths: God tells us we are the apple of his eye (Zech. 2:8), that our worth is far above rubies (Prov. 31:10), that he even knows the number of hairs on our heads (Luke 12:7), and that he rejoices over us with singing (Zeph. 3:17).

Your value in God's eyes makes the Hope Diamond look like a gum ball trinket. —JOANNE KRAFT

So, What Are You Really Worth?

It's the creator or owner of a thing that determines its value, marking the price and deciding its worth. Our value is in the hands of our Creator. We were created by him and for him (Col. 1:16). Paul reminds us in 1 Corinthians 6:20 and again in 1 Corinthians 7:23, "You were bought with a price" (NRSV). The redeeming love of Christ paid our eternal ransom. Heavenly currency personally handed over by the bloodstained hands of Jesus to his Father for your very soul.

Charles Spurgeon once said, "Redeeming love is the theme of Heaven. When you reach the upper realms, your most important memory will not be that you were wealthy or poor in this life, nor the fact that you sickened and died, but that you were 'bought with a price.'"[5]

Yet, daily, we are spiritually rocked to sleep. We believe the whispers of the world. *You aren't special. Your life really isn't all that important. Nobody loves you. You're worthless.* We are unaware or not understanding that God marked our price on Calvary. And because of that blessed day, God sees us through holy spectacles of his only son's worth. What kind of love is this? A love beyond measure.

If we struggle to understand our worth, it's because we don't understand Christ's worth. —JOANNE KRAFT

Samuel's friend lost his biological family and his perception of value. The Lord placed this child in a foster home with parents who know his value and believe he is worth so much more. They've now adopted him.

Do your children know what they're worth? If they're struggling with this concept, could it be you are, too? Do you need a remedial lesson to understand your value? Or is God's Word enough? The next time you attempt to put a price tag on your life—for what it's worth, you're worth more.

Like I said in the beginning of this chapter, bullies have been around for centuries. As a mean mom raising children in the twenty-first century, I may not be able to intercept every painful experience meant to harm my little ones, but I can teach my children how much they're worth and to be strong and stand strong against whatever Goliath threatens to harm them.

Mom to Mom

How do you protect your child from bullies?

℮ Bullying is a harsh reality. My daughter is a victim. I don't want my child to hide from life, but I don't want to keep sending her to a school where people continually attempt to crush her spirit. I have long told her that she is the only one with the power over her feelings, but that's a hard concept for a fourteen-year-old to understand. —EVA STOCKTON

℮ The world is chock full of bullies. We have to give our kids the power to defend themselves. —JESSICA KING

℮ We explain to our children what bullying "looks like" because it's not necessarily beating up on someone. It can also be mean intentions to hurt someone either physically or emotionally. With social media being so prevalent, we also talk about how bullying can also take place online. I remind them of 1 Peter 3:8 (NLT): "Finally, all of you should be of one mind. Sympathize with each other. Love each other as brothers and sisters. Be tenderhearted, and keep a humble attitude."

It is important to teach kids not to bully, but to stick up for others who are unable. "You must teach people to have genuine love, as well as a good conscience and true faith" (1 Tim. 1:5 CEV). —KELLA PRICE

⟋My son, Chris, was not a liar; he didn't stir up stuff. He was a pretty passive kid—which meant *target*. There'd been incidents at school. I started to notice he was depressed and wasn't acting himself. I decided to take time off of work to meet him directly after school to pick him up. I witnessed the kids kicking his backpack as he was trying to make his way from his last class to my car. I was horrified. But it got me to take a stand for him and change his school. See, kids don't have much power. We are the parent. We are their advocate. We know our children best. —KATIE CHANEY

Notes

[1] Lina Das, "Sandra's Biggest Hitch," *Daily Mail,* July 14, 2009, www.dailymail.co.uk/home/you/article-1198116/Sandras-biggest-hitch.html.

[2] Justin Patchin, Joseph Schafer, and Sameer Hinduja, "Cyberbullying and Sexting—Law Enforcement Perceptions," *FBI Law Enforcement Bulletin,* June 2013, http://leb.fbi.gov/2013/june/cyberbullying-and-sexting-law-enforcement-perceptions.

[3] Consumer Reports, "That Facebook Friend Might Be 10 Years Old, and Other Troubling News," *Consumer Reports Magazine,* June 2011, www.consumerreports.org/cro/magazine-archive/2011/june/electronics-computers/state-of-the-net/facebook-concerns/index.htm.

[4] Joanne Kraft, "How Much Are You Worth?," *ParentLife,* April/May 2013.

[5] Charles H. Spurgeon, *Spurgeon's Sermons on the Death and Resurrection of Jesus* (Peabody, MA: Hendrickson Publishers, 2005), 194.

CHAPTER TWELVE

Mean Moms Don't Speak the Language of *Busy*

- -

Beware the barrenness of a busy life.
—**Socrates**

It's been said some twins share a secret language. The scientific term for this phenomenon is *idioglossia*. The dictionary defines this twin talk as a private form of speech invented by one child or children in close contact. It's a pathological condition characterized by speech so distorted as to be unintelligible. Google "twin talk" and you'll discover a YouTube video where two adorable toddlers communicate in joyful gibberish. It's fascinating to watch. They seem to understand each other perfectly.

My husband and I share a form of idioglossia, if you will. Since we both have police backgrounds, we talk in police lingo. When we don't want our children to know what we're saying, we pepper our conversation with police phonetics and criminal penal codes. After years of gang fights, armed robberies, and vehicle pursuits together, it was a way of communication that came quite naturally to us. Once we were married and had a few crumb crunchers of our own, we began to use our work language at home—a lot.

For example, if we were at McDonald's, and I happened to notice the children wandering off to sit at a table dangerously close to someone who looked like a kidnapper (don't you judge me; you've thought the very same thing about a shady character or two), I'd give a subtle head nod in the direction of the potential assailant and whisper to Paul, *207*, which he knew as the California Penal Code for the felony of kidnapping. Without another word, my husband would direct the children to sit somewhere else.

Our language came in quite handy when our silver Chevy Suburban was filled to the brim with all four kiddos. If I wanted to stop for an ice cream but didn't want the kids to hear what I was saying, I'd ask their father out loud, "Sweetheart, would you like to get an Ida-Charles-Edward Charles-Robert-Edward-Adam-Mary?" Only Paul understood the first letter in each word spelled out my request and would steer our car straight to the nearest Baskin Robbins.

Busy Moms Are Bilingual

I believe moms share a secret language as well—the language of busy. It's our very own form of idioglossia. Don't believe me? The next time you run into a girlfriend at the grocery store, I double dog dare you to have a conversation without using the B-word. I betcha a dollar you'll say *busy* more than once before you part.

No matter how many girlfriends I talk to in the bread aisle, no one seems to be sharing much joy in their busyness. I have yet to hear someone tell me, "My calendar is jam-packed and I couldn't be happier!"

How you spend your time is a flashing billboard—it tells your child what's important to you. —JOANNE KRAFT

Parents love their children passionately. We want to do more for them with every passing year and give them much more than we had as kids. In the Gospel of John, Jesus shares a warning with us that I believe has a powerful message for us busy moms. "The thief comes only to steal and kill and destroy. I came that they may have life and have it abundantly" (John 10:10 ESV).

It reminds me of an acronym a friend once shared with me: BUSY—burdened under Satan's yoke. I believe the enemy's first move is to steal our time. We all have time stealers in our lives. What's yours? If you're scratching your head in an attempt to figure it out, I can help. *Where would someone put a sticky note if she needed to get in touch with you immediately?* Would she put the note on your iPhone? Maybe she would leave a note on your TV, or possibly your laptop, or maybe your steering wheel?

Think about it.

The biggest time-sucking time stealer is easy to spot when you do this little exercise. If you're a real truth seeker, try asking someone in your family where he or she would put your note. I must warn you, though: the answer might smart a bit.

A mom came up to me after a weekend conference and said, "I loved this exercise you shared, Joanne. I asked my five-year-old son where he'd put a note for me and his daddy if he needed to get ahold of us in an emergency. You know what he said? He said, 'Mommy, I'd put your note on the kitchen counter, and I'd put Daddy's sticky note on the toilet seat.'"

The enemy's second shot is to kill our joy. Beth Moore once said, "No one can do a thousand things to the glory of God, and in our vain attempt to do so we stand to forfeit a precious thing."[1] I believe joy is a precious thing. If you'd peeked into my world as a young mom, I'm not sure you'd have seen much joy as I squawked when my kids lost a shin guard and barked when I was running late for something.

When joy is gone, we aren't too far away from Satan's kill shot to destroy our relationships. Busyness is the tool he uses, first to steal our time, then to kill our joy with his eye set on the prize of annihilating our relationships. Jesus warns us that the enemy comes to steal, kill, and destroy. Why wasn't I heeding this advice? Here's some real hard truth: busyness is not something to take lightly anymore.

Jesus wants to give us his abundance of peace from the chaos of a busy life. He says it's why he came, to give us abundant life. I want to take him up on that offer.

Frustration is not the will of God. There is time to do anything and everything God has called us to. —ELISABETH ELLIOT

Training Our Kids to Do What?

> Train a child up in the way he should go, and when he is
> old he will not depart from it. (Prov. 22:6 NKJV)

As Christian parents, we love to embrace the encouragement of Proverbs 22:6. But what if the way we train our children these days, the way we think they should go, is to become busier and busier? If that's the playing field they're growing up in, then we need to understand it's a life they may not depart from.

When a mean mom instills boundaries with activity, she won't consider busyness a feather in her cap. She sees a crazy, busy life as a potential time stealer, joy killer, and relationship destroyer. She refuses to glorify the bondage of busyness and is okay to live with the fact that her children may not like her when she tells them *no*— they can't add something else to their bulging schedules.

Holy Hibernation

After fifteen years at the pulpit, my pastor announced he was taking a few months' sabbatical. There may be some who might disagree with this decision.

"He's taking a sabbatical?"

"Pastors don't take time off."

Why not? God did.

I'll admit, when I heard the announcement I smiled to myself and thought, *I love this. Good for him. Everyone needs rest.* He was preaching to the choir. I wrote the book *Just Too Busy—Taking Your Family on a Radical Sabbatical*, remember?

For the life of me I don't understand why our world has us convinced the busier we are the more productive we are—the more valuable we are. It's a lie, plain and simple. Don't be tricked by the captivity of activity. You and I both need to be still and rest. We've been wired that way.

God's creatures take rest to a whole new level by hibernating each year. Most of us think of bears when we think of hibernation, yet bears aren't considered true hibernators since they birth their babies and care for them during the winter months. Badgers, groundhogs, wasps, rodents, and some fish species hibernate. They retreat and lie dormant, their heart rate and metabolism slowing to a snail's pace, readying them for another year.

In the Old Testament, God included Sabbath rest as a weekly command—which makes me think: *What if a sabbatical rest is like taking a holy hibernation?* Too often, we look at taking time off or being still as a sign of laziness or being unproductive. The truth is we're made to do great things for his glory. We can't accomplish his plans for our life without rest. It strengthens us for the holy job ahead.

Do you desire to raise your children into responsible, independent, God-honoring adults? That's quite a task. It's a lifetime occupation that takes daily rest. Children already keep us busy, so let's not self-sabotage our days and steal anointed opportunities to kick back and take a breather. What example are you giving your children if you never rest?

What Motivates a Busy Mom?

This may seem a silly question to some. I imagine a crowd of moms shouting in unison: "I live this crazy, busy life because I love my children!" Love is the motivating factor. We love our kids. Period. End of story. What better answer is there?

For busy moms, it isn't hard to encourage them to look around at their topsy-turvy schedules and realize changes need to be made. For others, it can be nothing more than, "It's just what we do. Every fall we sign the kids up for baseball, and every spring we sign the kids up for soccer."

There are a handful of other parents out there who enlist their children on teams and activities because they get their social dance card filled by other adults involved in the same activities. These are the moms I believe suffer from ADD—or as I like to call it, Activity Denial Disorder. Our marshmallow mom Delia Doestoomuch suffers from this malady. She's in denial of the true reason she's overwhelmed and overscheduled. Denial is a master manipulator. It tells all of us busy moms, "You're an awful mom if you don't give her singing lessons." Or, "Johnny just might be the next Derek Jeter—of course he should be playing year-round baseball."

Then there are the moms who live vicariously through their kids. I can relate a little bit. I really wanted a child who excelled in soccer. Four children, a dozen soccer seasons, and twenty-three years later, I never had that experience. I desired it more than they knew, but I didn't want to force my children to play when they were no longer interested, or manipulate their field time by coaching all their teams. No one wants to be *that* mom.

Dr. John J. Mangoli, author of *Avoiding the 15 Biggest Mistakes Parents Make*, shares this with his readers: "The topic of the child who is engaging in too many activities may seem insignificant. On the contrary though, it is very easy for well-meaning parents to overlook. I've had many a sick office visit for a child who is feeling tired and worn out. Parents and children both arrive at my office bewildered as to the cause." He goes on to make a plea: "Please let your children be involved in outside activities but don't live your interests through them. If you love a certain sport, rather than pushing it on your child, join a team yourself."[2]

Dr. Mangoli makes a good point. To help you navigate your day and put a little peace back into your life, I've included an acronym (PEACE) below. This list will help you remember what to do the next time you feel yourself drowning in the chaos or in bondage to your busyness.

- Pray. Hand your laundry list of have-tos into God's hands. Who better to set your priorities than him? Once you ask, then be still and know he is God (Ps. 46:10). His peace in prioritizing will help you move forward.
- Exercise *no*. Our family took a yearlong sabbatical from all extracurricular activities. I learned to say *no* to the captivity of activity that year. Our kids survived, and I have a feeling yours would, too.
- Ask someone older. Seek counsel from a parent or grandparent before adding to your activities. Who better to ask than someone who's been there? "A wise man will hear and increase learning, and a man of understanding will attain wise counsel" (Prov. 1:5 NKJV).

- Choose wisely. Pay attention to how much time, energy, and financial burden each activity brings. Pick and choose well. "Teach us to number our days, that we may gain a heart of wisdom" (Ps. 90:12).
- Excel in relationships. Author Andy Stanley says kids today are "experience rich and relationship poor."[3] Discover ways to bring your family close. Can't think of things to do? Google *family fun activities* or check out a book from the library.

Be Still Before He Makes You

> The LORD is my shepherd; I shall not want. He makes me to lie down in green pastures; He leads me beside the still waters. He restores my soul; He leads me in the paths of righteousness for His name's sake. (Ps. 23:1–3 NKJV).

Did you get that line back there? He *makes me* lie down.

What will it take to make you lie down? Will you be obedient and do it without being forced to? The Hebrew word used for "makes me lie down" is *rabats*, which means to recline or stretch out. Why in the world would I fight the opportunity to recline and stretch out? Yet, so often I do.

These days, I try to lie down before he gives me a holy time-out. I have come to crave his stillness, hunger for his refreshing, and delight in his restoration. Sadly, I think some moms are petrified of stillness and silence.

> I hear a lot of people say, "The fear of death and the fear of speaking are two of the main fears of my generation." But I disagree; I think it's the fear of silence. We refuse to turn off our computers, turn off our phones, log off Facebook and just sit in silence because in those

moments we might actually have to face up to who we really are. We fear silence like it's an invisible monster gnawing at us, ripping us open and showing us our dissatisfaction. Silence is terrifying.[4]

"Be still." If I had a nickel for each time I told my four children those two words, I'd be typing this chapter from a beachfront home in Maui. They are the very words God tells us, his own kids, in Psalm 46:10:

> Be still, and know that I am God;
> I will be exalted among the nations,
> I will be exalted in the earth! (NKJV)

I lost the ability to *be still* somewhere along the road of marriage and my first toddler. When Jesus calms the storm in the Gospel of Mark, he says, "Peace, be still." If you need more peace in your life, learning to *be still* is how you'll get some back.

When our son David was a toddler, he refused to go to sleep. Our bright idea was to drive him to sleep. Yes, desperation won out. His daddy became his limo driver and cruised around town until David nodded off. Sometimes hours would go by before I'd see the flash of headlights through my kitchen window announcing their return. (Chevron has us to thank for their fiscal year of 1998.)

I'd open the front door as Paul carried in our exhausted little boy, limp from slumber and slung over his daddy's shoulder. No matter how many nights this father-and-son car ride occurred, his daddy shared incredulous antics of a little boy who would stay busy doing anything but be still. "He touches buttons on his car seat, flicks the window, and even kicks the passenger seat in front of him until finally I have to lean it forward out of his reach. Once I remove anything and everything that might distract him, he finally nods off."

Many of us have the same problem. Our lives are so busy we're overstimulated and distracted. We don't know how to be still. It doesn't feel natural. We're in captivity to our activity and have no clue how to slow down. Here are a few things that worked for me:

- Remove any activity from your calendar that your husband has complained about over and over again. How about you listen to him this time? Let it go!
- Stop driving everywhere. How many hours are you spending in your car? How about setting a mileage limit for the week? The price of gas alone is enough to help curb your job as a domestic cab driver.
- Time-out—it's not just for kids. Turn off the TV. Turn off your phone. Make yourself a cup of tea and meditate on a Scripture or just sit in silence. Why not give God the chance to talk to you today?

In the hustle and bustle of our much-too-connected world, we drown out stillness. When we are still, God's Word promises we can feel his presence and know he is God. My pastor is giving the good example of taking a sabbatical rest before God makes him take one. He is leading his church in a posture of refreshment and modeling holy hibernation. Why? To come back stronger for his God-ordained tasks ahead.

Before you add your name or your child's name to anything more, stop and ask yourself why you're really doing it. If you are feeling stretched in a million directions or completely overwhelmed, remember that's not from God. Jesus tells us his yoke is easy and his burden is light. Jesus is not the Prince of Burdensome Busyness. He is the Prince of Peace.

Mom to Mom

How does a mean mom tame busyness?

℮⁀We limit to one extracurricular a semester and one social weekend night out—so they can spend either Friday or Saturday with their friends, but not both! We constantly emphasize family and the importance and value of spending time together. —STEPHANIE DICKINSON

℮⁀How do I keep from being swallowed up by the busy life? God called me first and foremost to be a mom. Especially in this season with small kids at home, I am a mom first. The other things in my life (writing, marketing, etc.) must all come after that. For me it's a daily struggle . . . a daily choice to put first things first and let other things slide. —LINDSEY BELL

℮⁀We have four children, ages seven and under, and we have just now let our oldest start trying out different sports. We've had friends over the years that start their kids in soccer as soon as they turn three years old. Those kids have no idea if they even like soccer, and the parents are wearing themselves out by running their child to a number of practices and games each week. When you start adding siblings to the mix, do the math. Two practices a week and then a game every Saturday is bad enough for a three-year-old. Add a couple kids to that, and it's downright crazy! —AUDREY HANCHETT

℮⁀I say *no* more often lately because of past guilt/mistakes/bad attitude I'd have when so busy. We limit our kids' activities, and we have family discussions about the commitments that I say yes to at the church and school because it often means something at home will go to back burner that week. —NICOLE HAMILTON

❧I try to limit my "going out" to one day during the week. Just being on the go all the time makes me feel busy! So I stack my errands and shopping on one day. It helps my younger kids at home stick to more of a routine, too. —AMY POTRATZ

❧I'm a working mom with one child, so I have to be selective about the number of activities. I'm thankful her school offers after-school art class and music. I also taught my daughter early the gift of relaxation and creative play. She is perfectly content to stay home and read for hours, or draw so Mommy can get stuff done around the house, or just have cuddle time. The days can be long, but the years are short! —DEANN OKAMARA

Notes

[1] Beth Moore and Dale McCleskey, *To Live Is Christ: Embracing the Passion of Paul* (Nashville, TN: Broadman & Holman Publishers, 2001).

[2] John J. Mangoli, "Too Many Activities," in *Avoiding the 15 Biggest Mistakes Parents Make* (Charleston, SC: Booksurge, 2007), 15–16.

[3] Andy Stanley and Reggie Joiner, *Parental Guidance Required: Study Guide* (Sisters, OR: Multnomah, 2004), 64.

[4] Jefferson Bethke, *Jesus > Religion: Why He Is So Much Better Than Trying Harder, Doing More, and Being Good Enough* (Nashville, TN: Thomas Nelson, 2013).

CHAPTER THIRTEEN

Mean Moms Mean Business

– –

Your greatest contribution to the kingdom of God
may not be what you do but who you raise.
—Andy Stanley

I f you walk into any Christian bookstore, you can't swing your purse without hitting a book on grace: *Grace-full Parenting, Gardening with Grace, Cooking with Grace, Grace-Based Car Repair*. Grace defined biblically is unmerited, undeserving favor.

I don't want to trivialize the most powerful message behind the work of Jesus on the cross. There is nothing I can ever do to deserve salvation and eternal life. It's by grace I have been saved and not of works, lest I boast, the Scripture tells us (Eph. 2:8–9).

There's no doubt, as far as parenting is concerned, that grace in a moment deserving of painful correction has the power to change a life. God knows this full well. Years ago, when I was a young girl, my mother sent me to my bedroom to wait for my father to get home from work. I'd been sent to my personal holding cell until my punishment was meted out. It wasn't long until I heard our front door open, mumblings of my parents' voices, and the heavy footsteps belonging to my Teamster, truck-driving father as he strode toward my bedroom. I don't recall the offense, but I do recall my punishment was deserving of a spanking. But my father did something I'll never forget. He proceeded to give my toy box a few swats instead. I was spared.

Grace made a difference for me that day. Forty years later, I know grace can be the greatest teacher when the pupil is the most undeserving. God's greatest gift is grace, and I know of some who use it well with their children.

Unfortunately, a marshmallow mom will sometimes use it as her excuse not to discipline when it's hard. God creates limits and boundaries to guide and protect. When we step over the line he's drawn, he often responds with discipline. The same follow-through is needed with our own children. Our kids will never learn if we fail to provide needed correction to teach them a different way. If we ignore discipline and just hope they figure things out, the next boundary we give will be disregarded.

I've known a few Christian parents who fall like martyrs on their swords of mercy and grace. I am not a junkyard dog when it comes to discipline; I take my cues from a loving God who put boundaries in place to protect me, correct me, and direct me.

Definition of the Word

Before we get started on ways to discipline your child, we need to start with the definition of the word.

> **dis•ci•pline** *noun* \ˈdi-sə-plən\
> Definition: regimen, training
> Synonyms: conduct, cultivation, curb, development, education, exercise, method, practice, preparation, self-control, self-government, self-mastery, self-restraint

My favorites? Cultivation. Development. Education. Self-mastery. The Bible explains the word *discipline* this way: the Hebrew word *muwcar* occurs fifty times in fifty verses in the Hebrew concordance of the King James Version, and it is defined most often as instruction (thirty times), correction (eight times), chasten (four times), and chastisement (three times).

Discipline, in a nutshell, is mainly used two ways: to educate by instruction, which is the lion's share of the meaning when used in the Bible, and to develop or to correct and chasten. This is the punishment portion of discipline, which occurs only three times by definition in God's Word. Both kinds of discipline mold a child into an adult, like a potter molds his clay.

Developing a child takes time and one size does not fit all. I have four children and each one is different from the next. It takes trial and error and much love to do it well. In time, a parent and a child learn what works.

> *Developing a child takes time and one size does not fit all.*

How Not to Discipline

When you pick up a mean mom parenting book, I imagine some of you were expecting a pretty vicious discipline chapter. If that's the case, then you and your child both need a refresher in what *mean* really means.

A mean mom desires to raise her kids biblically, which means she follows what God has to say about it:

> Fathers, do not provoke your children, lest they become discouraged. (Col. 3:21 NKJV)

The word *provoke* means we're not to exacerbate a difficult situation or exasperate our children. There are quite a few ways we provoke our children—sometimes without being aware of it—and I've included some of them here.

Delay. Correcting your children should be swift. It's passive-aggressive to hold a wrong they've done over their head for an extended amount of time—not to mention cruel. Don't say: "Go to your room and wait until your father gets home." That's torture to a child. Sitting in your bedroom and watching the clock tick-tock at a snail's pace, all the while thinking of the thousands of ways your dad might respond—no thanks.

> *Please don't expect perfection. There should be buckets of grace given to a child who is trying very hard to grow up.*

Make a misdemeanor a felony. Children are learning as they're growing. They will make lots of mistakes along the way. Please don't expect perfection. There should be buckets of grace given to a child who is trying very hard to grow up. Your children give cues to how they see you as a disciplinarian; watch how they respond the next time they spill a glass of milk or break one of your favorite dishes. Their response is a direct result of yours.

Be ridiculous. How often have you threatened with the ridiculous? Admit it. You've said some pretty silly things over the years, haven't you?

The next time you pinch your sister, I'm going to send you to bed without dinner—for a month!

If you don't eat your broccoli, you're going to sit there all night until you do.

Turn on your video game without asking one more time, and I'll throw it away.

Sass me like that again, and I'll feed your tongue to wild birds!

You'll stay in your room until your attitude changes or
until Jesus returns.

ᴗᴗ

The Bible says let your *yes* be *yes* and your *no* be *no*. Say what you mean and mean what you say. Speak words of truth when you correct your child (Matt. 5:37).

Be inconsistent. The backbone of discipline is consistency. Every. Single. Time. This is what separates a mean mom from her marshmallow mom girlfriend. Think first before setting a boundary. Don't yell or shout threats you have no intention of following through with. Better yet, don't yell or shout at all.

Shout. I was raised by a family of shouters. We're a passionate bunch. Everything is over the top, including the volume of our voices. I remember sitting in a Bible study when one of the women shared, "Yelling means you've lost control of the situation."

One mean mom had this to say: "Communicate with your husband long before you discipline the kids. It's more effective to agree on a strategy together before it's handed to the child. It's always best if you're both on the same page. If it becomes a power struggle, then you should go back to the drawing board away from the child and restrategize."

Respond or react. We talked about this in Chapter Seven—"Mean Moms Don't Take Sides." When I'm prepared, I don't react. And, may I add, if I'm red-hot angry, I react every time. God-honoring discipline is responsive, not reactionary. Here's a simple definition of what we produce in each case.

React. Shouting. Yelling. Screaming. Stomping. Crying. Throwing things. Hurtful words. Discouraging words. Shaming a child. Guilting a child. Reactionary discipline is ineffective to create lasting change. The only thing reacting does is shine a light on my poor behavior—and teach my child to act the same way.

Respond. Even-tempered communication. Eye contact and follow-through. Prepared and planned decisions. Grace when least deserved. Justice and mercy. Forgiveness. Responsive discipline instructs and creates growth opportunities to direct children toward the purpose and plans God has for them.

In our home, discipline is enacted differently depending on whether the issue is moral or non-moral. Non-moral issues like forgetting to feed the dog are dealt with differently than moral issues like lying, deceit, stealing, disrespect, or physically harming another. In the case of lying, a moral issue, we give a child a chance to be honest before correction, and if he or she is truthful, there is grace. This grace can help children to understand the value of honesty. That it's safe to tell the truth. Here are a few age-appropriate tools that work wonders:

- *Time-out.* Keep it short. One minute per year of a child's age. Use a timer and restart the time if they defiantly get up or walk away. Make sure to turn off the TV and anything else that may distract or entertain. Time-outs work best when used with a child between two and eight years old.
- *Spank.* According to Dr. James Dobson, it should be used in the case of open defiance or an action that could bring harm. Like when my son was three and ran out into oncoming traffic after I told him to stand beside me. This is the last tool in your mom toolbox. Never use this method in anger, and if you were raised in an abusive home, you may not understand healthy limits. If that's the case, I'd recommend not using this tool at all.
- *Restrict privileges.* Warn once. Then remove an item your child would miss—a toy, a planned trip to the

park, TV, electronics. Younger children will feel the sting after a few minutes to a few hours. Consider restriction lasting a few days to a few weeks with your preteen to teenager.

- *Natural consequences.* Don't like what I made for dinner? It's okay. Going to bed hungry is a natural consequence. If your child turns down your request to wear a coat on a windy day, being chilly for a bit is a natural consequence, too. Allow them to happen. They are wonderful teachers.

When Paul and I met, we had a lot in common. One of those things was our love of police work. With this early passion came the big mistake of seeing a lot of things in black and white. Working in a high-crime community, well, it gets that judgment muscle as strong as steel. As young parents, we transferred some of those learned behaviors into our home.

She didn't make her bed—for the second day in a row? Yep. That's a chore felony.
He sassed me in front of my girlfriend? Felony.
She got a C- on her science exam? A felony for sure.

Discipline loses its teaching power when you treat every infraction like a capital-punishment offense. What I'd give for a dozen do-overs in my younger parenting years. I'd watched so many parents make mistakes I didn't want to repeat, so I believed coming down hard was the right way much too often. If I could turn back the clock, I'd live by this code of law.

First Offense
Grace, undeserving favor, and communication almost every time.

Second Offense
Infraction. Just like a parking citation, there'd be disciplinary action, along with just enough consequence to feel a sting.

Third Offense
Misdemeanor. A misdemeanor offense is a probationary period. Consequences include a working detail or rights taken away; all the while, the kids can earn back privileges with good behavior. For a teenager, this could be a cell phone, Internet access, TV time, friend time— you get the picture.

As harsh as it may sound when I put discipline into the form of police work, it's how lots of parents still parent today. Firstborn children know this very well. We are the guinea pigs (as my dad told me), so everything is uncharted waters. Thankfully, we have the opportunity to ask our children for forgiveness when we treat an infraction like a misdemeanor or a misdemeanor like a felony.

Asking a child to forgive you is a humbling opportunity to teach your child you're not perfect and that you make mistakes, too. It opens wide the door to communication and maybe even the place to share why you reacted the way you did. My mother died of lung cancer, so if my children began smoking, I'd have to overcome the impulse to give them life without the possibility of parole!

Grace-FULL Parenting
Like I said earlier, grace should not be the excuse for a marshmallow mom who doesn't want to deal with a problem, but grace will

always be God's greatest lesson for me to follow. My friend Jessica Wolstenholm is an author and ministry leader at GraceforMoms. com. She recently shared a wonderful lesson with me about parenting with grace:

~~ ~~ ~~

She ran her toothbrush under the faucet, then placed it back in the holder, all this while her dad and I stood there. Was my five-year-old about to deceive us while we watched?

"Did you brush your teeth?" I asked.

"Uh-huh," she hesitantly replied.

"You did?" I asked to be sure.

"No," she admitted. And I felt fire well up in the pit of my stomach as I realized this is probably not the first time she's pretended to brush her teeth.

"Brush your teeth right now and then go get in your bed," I sternly directed, to give me time to compose myself.

Five minutes later in her bed, my favorite place to have peace-filled conversations of faith and teaching moments, I felt the Lord calm my spirit as he led me to engage in a grace-filled, holy moment with my girl.

"Sweetie, that wasn't the first time you lied about brushing your teeth, is it?"

"No." She was ashamed or maybe just embarrassed she got caught.

"Hope, when you've lied about it, did something inside you tell you not to do it? Did you get an icky feeling in your heart that maybe it was wrong?"

She shyly nodded her head.

"Sweetie, that was Jesus. Because he lives in your heart, he will tell you when you are about to make a wrong choice. From now on, I want you to listen to him when you feel him telling you what you are about to do is wrong, okay?"

"Okay," she muttered.

"But if we ever catch you lying about brushing your teeth or anything else again, there will be big trouble."

She understood.

⌒ ⌒ ⌒

Grace. I can see how God pours it over me, every time I make a wrong choice right in front of him. He gently corrects me and reminds me that he is there to redirect my path.

We want so badly to raise great kids that we vigilantly counter every wrong choice with a consequence, desiring to convince them to never do it again. And we must. We must let them experience discipline and the effects of their actions. But we must also allow them to experience grace, for in those experiences they will come to understand the One who covers every mistake and every bad choice.

There is no formula for knowing when to extend grace and when to deliver consequences. Sometimes it's one or the other. Sometimes it's both. We can only know how to respond in every situation by allowing the Holy Spirit to grab hold of us—and lead the way.

> Let us then approach God's throne of grace with
> confidence, so that we may receive mercy and find grace
> to help us in our time of need. (Heb. 4:16)

If you're a marshmallow mama, this chapter may be where your highlighter was the busiest. If you're a mean mom already, maybe there are a few areas you can tweak to encourage better results in your child. Either way, as long as love is the main ingredient, discipline will have the ability to assist God in molding your child into a great kid and eventually an adult you can be proud of.

Mom to Mom

How do you discipline your child?

〜I've tried everything, but I think the biggest thing is to remain consistent whatever method of discipline you choose. —JENNY SULPIZIO

〜I learned with my three kids that a certain way of disciplining may work with one but not another. Each child is an individual, and I've had to handle them that way. I have a friend who says parenting isn't something you do, it's a relationship. Just like any other relationship in my life, I have to relate to each child personally and individually. —LARA VAN HULZEN

〜I'm a single mean mama, so I have to be the heavy every time. I use a flyswatter! —CATHY SIMPKINS

〜I don't have children, but I teach a lot of them. One thing that made a huge impact on me growing up, and I use in the classroom now, is my mother's attitude. When she disciplined me, I knew I was loved unconditionally and unwaveringly. She made it clear it was my behavior/choices that were being disciplined. It was a great, affirming way to approach things. —MICHELLE MURRAY

〜Never threaten. Say something once without yelling. If there's no appropriate response, get immediately off your butt *without* anger, walk over and physically but gently guide child through correct response. Child-raising and discipline is the process of *walking alongside*. It is not a spectator sport. —DEBORAH SILVA

☙A mean mom is aligned with God's view of discipline and raising a child that considers others before themselves. It's having a firm and consistent position on how you will raise your children and not wavering to them or the pressures of society. Oftentimes that means walking the path less travelled or getting the cold shoulder for a while, but the results are worth it when you have a thriving child and eventually an adult. —CARMEN SUTHEIMER

CHAPTER FOURTEEN

Mean Moms Embrace Failure

- -

We need to embrace failure instead of trying to avoid it.
Those people who spend their lives trying to avoid
failure are also eluding maturity.

—Henry Cloud and John Townsend

"You're never going to believe what I saw today." My husband walked in the front door with a curious grin.

"What did you see?" I asked.

"A teenager was driving beside me, and I could see they had a ribbon hanging from their rearview mirror . . ."

"Wow, a ribbon? You're right. I wouldn't have guessed," I teased.

". . . a ribbon that said fifth place. I'm not even kidding—fifth place? Do we give out ribbons to everyone now? Have we become a people who celebrate mediocrity?" He mocked, "Johnny, congratulations on not doing very well. Here's your ribbon."

My husband was on a rant now. I knew I had to bring him down from the ledge, but I just had to poke him one more time.

167

"Well, maybe they received fifth place in the Boston Marathon. Now that would be impressive. Not everyone wins first place, Paul. Think about it, second place is still a very big deal in the Olympics."

"Joanne, you know what I think about second place."

Here it comes. The very words he taught all of the Kraft kids. I couldn't help but draw them out of him.

"Second place is just first loser." He winked.

There is a lot of truth to what my husband was saying. I've noticed it more and more in the schools our kids attend. Choosing one winner isn't as smiled upon as it used to be. Reasons fall under:

- The other kids might get their feelings hurt.
- I don't want them to feel bad when I sing the praises of another child.
- Every child needs to be encouraged.

So begins the everyone-is-a-winner mentality. We spoon-feed it to our kids and remind them of how great they are, inflating their egos like hot air balloons. By the time they're teenagers, they think they're incredible and awesome. Unfortunately, when they become adults, they discover the hard way that they're not very incredible or awesome, just full of hot air.

This week, I received an email from my son's soccer coach. Apparently, the soccer league has a rule about winning by too many points. I didn't know rules like this existed: "Great game Saturday with the 7–0 victory! So you are aware, the league does have a rule to keep the games competitive. The rules state if you win by six or more goals, you lose points in the overall standings. You get points taken away for winning by six or more. . . ."

Seriously? Okay, let's be honest here. No one enjoys watching a team slaughtered on the field. Unless, of course, we're talking about the 2014 Super Bowl and the Seattle win over Denver. My husband is a huge fan and enjoyed every point made by his beloved Seahawks.

I digress.

As much as it stings to lose a game or two or all season long, a loss is a fabulous character-teaching opportunity. Losing means my child learns to be gracious to the winner, and most importantly, it fans the fire of ambition and hard work to maybe train a bit more. Better yet, when they do win, they've learned to get back up again after being knocked down.

I've been on a few last-place teams. My junior high soccer team, the Honeybees, lost every game but one during the two seasons I played for them. But, boy howdy, was that one win sweet. I learned more being on a losing team than I did on my high school championship team. I'd like to think my lessons in failure gave me the perseverance to work even harder next time.

Let Them Fall

Proctor and Gamble premiered a commercial at the 2014 Winter Olympics in Sochi, Russia. A two-minute photo montage set to music showed three mother-child relationships grow from infants into Olympian athletes. What makes this commercial so intriguing is that the scenes are snapshots of each little person falling down— an ice skater, a hockey player, and a downhill skier.

For though the righteous fall seven times, they rise again, but the wicked stumble when calamity strikes. (PROV. 24:16)

Over and over again, from infancy to adulthood, the viewer gets continual glimpses of each future medalist falling down again and again. The only person alongside them in each scene is their mother. We see the moms help their toddlers stand and, as the music plays, we watch these tiny athletes grow up with mom's consistent support. Finally, each mom watches from the stands as her grown-up child perfects their dream—to become an Olympian athlete. The commercial fades to black and one powerful sentence emerges: "For teaching us that falling only makes us stronger. Thank you, Mom."

Do you run in and make everything better, softening the blow of failure's teaching lesson? Mean moms don't.

Do you run in and make everything better, softening the blow of failure's teaching lesson? Mean moms don't. Marshmallow moms believe any kind of hurt should be avoided, so they coddle and co-depend.

Heidi's daughter went door-to-door selling cookies in the neighborhood. It's understandable a mom might want to tag along at a distance. But instead, this mom feared her daughter's failure and not only walked up to each door, but she gave the cookie pitch for her junior high girl—failure was not an option. If this mom only knew the teachable moments she was stealing from her child.

When was the last time you let your child fail?

- Sarah forgot her lunch—for the second time this month. Do you jump in the car and drop it off, *again*?
- Michael said he was sick when his friend called because he didn't want to play outside. His friend stops by to check how he's feeling. Do you go along with your son's lie?
- Jessica has had an after-school job—for the past two years. She passed her driver's license test this week but doesn't have any money saved for a car. She spent her income on fun things like clothes and movies. Do you give up your car so she can use it?

- Andrew tells you on Sunday that he needs items for a big school project due Monday. Do you cancel your plans and run to the store?

Debbie Glasser, PhD, believes a little failure can make a big difference in helping your child succeed: "If you want to help your kids succeed in school and feel more confident, focus on the upside of failure."[1]

Researchers found that students are more likely to succeed when parents and teachers simply reassure them that trying—and sometimes failing—is part of how we learn. This study further suggests that there's a vicious cycle taking place in the classroom. Instead of seeking new information with enthusiasm and interest, many children are afraid to fail, so they're reluctant to challenge themselves. What's more, they often assume tasks should come easy to them. If new tasks aren't mastered quickly, students may be quick to give up and quick to assume they aren't capable. When fear of failure keeps kids from trying to tackle difficult problems, the learning process is disrupted and self-confidence can take a hit.[2]

Betsy Shaw competed in the 1998 Olympic Winter Games of Nagano, Japan. It was the first time women's snowboarding was included in the game's history. Betsy fell more times than she cares to remember and came home *without* a medal. She, too, believes failure is an important element for a child's development.

One of the most rewarding parts of parenting or coaching or teaching kids for me is being able to talk about my failures. Some kids were shocked to learn that failure was part of the process of reaching the top. I love seeing the look on their faces when I tell them I had one World Cup season where I crashed in every single race I entered, but I didn't stop trying.

It's not just kids who need to learn about failure. When I came home from the Olympics, I was surprised at how many grown adults were hesitant to ask me about it. They were very quick to assume I was devastated and disappointed that I didn't win. Some of them seemed more pained by my crash than I was. I realized then that not everyone has been so regularly intimate with failure.[3]

> *Failure is not a thing to fear. It's a part of the process to success.*

Failure is not a *thing* to fear. It's a part of the process to success. Thomas Edison, the American inventor, was never intimidated by failure. He boasted, "I failed my way to success." After attending public school for a total of twelve weeks, he was deemed a dullard and a hyperactive child who was prone to distraction. His teacher called him *difficult*. His mother quickly pulled him from school and taught him at home. When he died at the age of eighty-three, the US patent office had over one thousand of his patents on file.[4]

Edison experienced a lifetime of failures, but he never saw failing in that light, *pardon the pun*. He helped develop Morse code and invented the light bulb, the phonograph, and moving pictures . . . to name a few.

Don't Steal a Pinch

While I was writing at my girlfriend's cabin, Sally, her eighty-year-old neighbor, came over and asked me if I'd like to go for a walk.

"Boy, would I." I was looking for any distraction to take my face out of my manuscript for a few minutes.

"How's the book coming, Joanne?" she asked, the click of her walking stick keeping rhythm with our steps.

"I'm concerned what I want to share may step on some toes. I want to encourage moms. I don't want to hurt anyone." I kept my eyes straight ahead on the road.

"Oh, Joanne, sometimes a little pinch now and then is a good thing."

Failure does not mean disaster for your child. It's a pinch, a small taste of pain that grows our kids into mature adults who when they fall stand again and again and again. Henry Cloud and John Townsend, authors of *Boundaries*, call it *safe suffering*.[5]

People who are growing up are drawn to individuals who wear battle scars, worry furrows, and tear marks on their faces. Their lessons can be trusted much more than the unlined faces of those who have never failed—and so have never truly lived. —JOHN TOWNSEND

Encouragement When They Fall

According to an article in the *Christian Post*, many young adults today are experiencing a *quarter-life crisis* (like a midlife crisis): there's a huge letdown if they're not in a fulfilling job or making a certain amount of money by the age of twenty-five. Biblical counselor June Hunt encourages parents to instill an understanding that "success isn't an exact amount of money, the perfect spouse, popularity in the arts, or the ability to achieve things." Instead, she argues, "success is becoming the person God created you to be."[6]

The positive lessons failure can bring to a child are immeasurable. I've included two big ones here.

Lesson One: Failure Doesn't Mean God's Abandoned You

God doesn't promise we will get everything we've ever wanted. Remind your children of the apostles in the Bible. Not one lived a fail-proof existence, yet all suffered for the gospel and were used mightily. The Lord is with us in our standing and in our falling, until the end of the ages (Matt. 28:20), and he will never leave us or forsake us (Heb. 13:5).

Lesson Two: God Promises Refreshment to Those Who Follow Him

God refreshes us in the midst of our trial. Remind your son or daughter that his or her hard work is not overlooked by God. He is the one who will give rest (Matt. 11:28–30). When their disappointment has them stuck wondering *why*, it's a great time to remind them to trust. There are things we may never understand this side of heaven, but God still directs us when we fall (Prov. 3:5–6).

The pain our children experience from falling and failing is a more powerful teacher than their mountaintop moments. Refrain from protecting them from the pinch of disappointment. When you smother a fiery trial, you steal a victorious moment from your child. God's amazing grace is supernatural and keeps any failure from being final.

Mom to Mom

What mean moms think about failure.

As a society, we no longer give the children the opportunity to learn from failing. We swoop in to make everything better. —SARA MUNDAY

 I never want anyone to feel bad or be upset, especially my kids. They would share with me something that upset them, and I would tell them you really don't feel like that, everything is fine. I taught my kids to deny their feelings—EPIC FAIL! I've learned over the last three years that it's okay if they are sad or upset. Now, I allow my kids to work though their issues with my help only if needed and by request. —SUSAN CLEARY

 My generation of parents were part of the *baby on board* movement where everything had padded corners and everyone got a trophy so nobody would get hurt or feel bad. —CHERI GREGORY

 A mean mom doesn't like to see her children fail or hurt any more than any other mom; she is just wise enough to understand her job is to teach—and sometimes that means letting a child fail. —EVA CHRISTIAN

Notes

[1] Debbie Glasser, "A Little Failure Can Make a Big Difference in Helping Your Child Succeed," *Psychology Today* website, March 26, 2012, www.psychologytoday.com/blog/parenting-news-you-can-use/201203/little-failure-can-make-big-difference-in-helping-your-child-.

[2] Ibid.

[3] Betsy Shaw, "Failure Is Good for Kids," *BabyCenter* blog, March 26, 2012, http://blogs.babycenter.com/mom_stories/0326201failure-is-good-for-kids.

[4] "Thomas Alva Edison," Biography.com website, accessed April 12, 2014, www.biography.com/people/thomas-edison-9284349#final-years&awesm=~oFF1z9xwXxIj0D.

[5] Henry Cloud and John Townsend, *Boundaries* (Grand Rapids, MI: Zondervan, 1992).

⁶ Tyler O'Neil, "Millennials Suffering Their Own Style of Mid-Life Crisis? 6 Biblical Lessons to Provide Comfort," *The Christian Post*, September 13, 2013, www.christianpost.com/news/millennials-suffering-their-own-style-of-mid-life-crisis-six-biblical-lessons-to-provide-comfort-104446.

CHAPTER FIFTEEN

Mean Moms Rule Technology

- -

We are digital immigrants while our children are digital natives.
—Tracey Eyster

*I*f your kids are awake, they're probably online. A study done by the Kaiser Family Foundation revealed that children between the ages of eight and eighteen spend an average of seven waking hours a day with technology.[1] With our worldwide appetite for iPads, iPods, smartphones, and the next shiny techno gadget to emerge, parents need to be vigilant and instill boundaries along the way.

When I polled my focus group of mean moms, technology ranked number one when it came to dialogue about instilling healthy rules at home. They have lots to say. The consensus was this: all of us want to understand what to do to keep our children safe. Many moms have done their best to delay cell phones and iPads, but many more have accepted this new way of life. The majority agreed technology is a big issue at home, and the biggest eye-opener was just how many of us have children who have been burned by it.

Technology has brought helpful apps to teach our kids everything from math and reading to eating your veggies. (The Prisoner of Carrot Castle is a favorite children's app of mine, by the way.) But the immense benefits have been muddied by easy access to pornography, violence, and mature content we don't want touching our children. When I sat in a youth ministry meeting recently, the guest speaker was from our local pregnancy crisis center and shared statistics about children and online use that made my stomach churn. "Eight is the average age a child sees pornography for the first time." Eight!

One mean mom had this to say, "My son was exposed to porn after innocently attempting to watch a skateboard video on YouTube. My daughter signed up for a little pre-tweeny-bopper site that her friends were also on. It was actually a site where you ask other people on there to become your boyfriend or girlfriend. We revoked her use of the site. After sneaking behind our backs to go on there again, the computer is no longer an option for her unless it's school-related" (Jenny Sulpizio).

Another mean mom shared her heartache over her son's battle with pornography. "Looking back, we weren't checking up on his online usage enough. When our son was in middle school, he found things online he shouldn't. This is a *great kid*, saved since he was nine, no problems, no issues, fun, serving God. Our trust level was high. He didn't tell us about his struggle until a year or so ago (he is seventeen now) and even now it's hard for him. Thankfully, God dealt with his heart and his sin. He shares his story with anyone he thinks needs to hear it. Most of the time now, he voluntarily leaves his phone upstairs at night with us, and we routinely talk with him and check his phone and our computers. He set up his own accountability with friends and other adult men. All this to say, set the rules early—check your kids' phones and talk to them about all this technology. Mostly, stay involved in their lives and in their business. It matters."

Parents must educate themselves on all things digital. Just as parents once protected their children from the unknowns of the wild west, so must we protect our children from the unknowns in the digital landscape. —TRACEY EYSTER

Ministry leaders Dennis and Barbara Rainey keep Psalm 101:2–4 taped to the top of their TV. A good verse to keep taped to our technology as well, if you ask me.

I will behave wisely in a perfect way.
Oh, when will You come to me?
I will walk within my house with a perfect heart.
I will set nothing wicked before my eyes;
I hate the work of those who fall away;
It shall not cling to me.
A perverse heart shall depart from me;
I will not know wickedness. (PS. 101:2-4 NKJV)

Dr. Aric Sigman, a leading psychologist, said:

> The problem with this generation is that we accept there should be limits on the consumption of many things, such as sunlight or sugar and salt, but screen time is not something that is thought of as consumption. It is important to impose boundaries, rules and limits.

What parents often assume is a benign pastime is their main waking activity and the sheer amount of time that children spend at screens can lead to increased risk of physical disease as well as psychosocial issues.[2]

It's fascinating to hear us mean moms talk. We're tough on protecting home computers with parental monitoring software and setting boundaries like no TV or Internet in the bedroom, yet we hand our children smartphones with little protection. The Swiss army knife of technology, a smartphone is a compact laptop and gives our kids full access to mature content, violent movies, and any adult pornography site or app they can get their hands on. It's natural that as children grow, their curiosity about sex grows, too. The scary thing is, by putting a miniature computer in their hands, we give not only good things, but we allow full access to a flood of damaging visual images and sinister temptations.

The Swiss army knife of technology, a smartphone is a compact laptop and gives our kids full access to mature content, violent movies, and any adult pornography site or app they can get their hands on.

She Is a Great Kid

Hope is a great kid. A daughter of a mean mom, she purchased her iPod with money she'd saved. The apps she put on her phone were harmless enough, or so her mom thought.

When Hope searched YouTube for music videos, she discovered more than she bargained for. One year later, heartbroken and full of shame, Hope confided to her youth group leader about her dirty little secret. When she sheepishly confessed her struggle and later shared her story with other little girls her age, they responded by clapping.

They understood and, later, a young girl approached Hope to share her own painful journey.

"My big brother told me and my friends, 'I have a surprise for you.' And showed us things on his phone my mom and dad would have never wanted us to see."

No one wakes up addicted to pornography. It's a slow fade. When Dr. James Dobson met with serial killer Ted Bundy, hours before his execution, Bundy confirmed the role pornography played in his life. "Pornography can reach out and snatch a kid from any house today. It snatched me out of my house twenty to thirty years ago. . . . "

Be careful little eyes what you see.
It's the second glance that ties your hands as
darkness pulls the strings. —"SLOW FADE," BY CASTING CROWNS

Smartphone Need or Want?

Having a phone to reach me in case of an emergency is a valid argument, in my opinion. But in the last ten years, in how many emergencies have my children used their phones to contact me? Zero. It got me thinking: Is a phone a need or a want?

One marshmallow mom gave her most passionate smartphone debate with her mean mom girlfriend. I call it the *kidnapper defense*. I overheard a mean mom ask her, "Is this the only reason you think he should have one, because he could be kidnapped?"

This marshmallow mom was honest and threw in, "Well, I also hate the kids looking like outcasts."

"What you're telling me is, not having a cell phone makes them lepers in society."

"I'd just feel safer if they had one. You know, like when they walk home from school."

"But our kids don't walk home from school. They take the bus."

"Well, then when they walk home from the bus stop."

"The bus stop is two blocks from your front door. And no one has been kidnapped in our neighborhood ever."

"Stop being so logical," she complained. "How about when they go to the mall with friends, how about then? Child molesters hang out at malls. I hear stories on the news all the time."

"Okay, not sure what local news you're watching, but if it makes you feel better, let him borrow your phone when he goes to the mall."

We fear kidnappers and homicidal maniacs when statistics are clear the real thing we should fear is what can reach our children through the Internet.

Logic is not a marshmallow mom's friend. In her heart of hearts, she wants her children to be safe and included. The last thing she wants is to keep a phone out of their hands and tattoo "outcast" on their forehead. Today, so many kids have smartphones, kids see it as a punishment when they don't have one, too. We fear kidnappers and homicidal maniacs when statistics are clear the real thing we should fear is what can reach our children *through* the Internet. The question remains: Is this technology your child is begging and pleading for a want or a need? Only you can answer that.

Back in My Day

The *back in my day* argument loses with kids because there really isn't anything to compare to a cell phone today. We don't buy our kids smartphones or cell phones, which makes them think we're pretty *old school*.

"Mom, do you remember the biggest change in technology when you were a child?"

"A pager."

"What's a pager?"

I was happy he asked. Finally I could share the technology of *my day* with him. "It was really cool. It was a small black box that clipped to your belt buckle—no bigger than a deck of cards," I bragged. "So, if someone wanted to get a hold of you, their phone number would light up on your pager, and then you'd know to call them." I smiled in the rearview mirror, pretty proud of myself.

Samuel stared at me for a moment. Awkward silence filled the car.

"Are you serious?" he laughed. "Let me get this straight . . . it *alerts* you that someone *wants* to call you (more laughter), so then you can go *find a phone* . . . to call them?"

"Well, young man, the '80s rocked. If my generation was so embarrassing, why did your generation remake all our music and claim it as theirs?"

Samuel wasn't about to be distracted. Laughing, he struggled to continue. "A monthly fee to *alert you* when somebody is calling—you're not even able to call them?" He was in full hysterics now and I wanted to karate chop him.

"Yeah, I wish I was alive in the 1900s—so I could be *alerted*."

"1980s!"

"Well, Mom, thank you very much for introducing me to your technology—a pager, *coming soon to a Goodwill near you*," he whispered.

Technology Addiction

How do you know if your child is addicted to technology? Well, how upset are they when you tell them, "It's time your iPod/ iPad/ laptop/cell phone needs a breather"? If you explain, "Your dad and I have decided to give technology a time-out for a while—and that includes your cell phone," how does your child respond?

Our daughter Grace was using her iPod to text her friends. When I realized this technology was her newest appendage and even slept with her at night, I suggested, "How about we put it to bed in my room? It can charge there." She responded like an alcoholic who discovered only water would be served.

After a while without it, she could see the problem she was having with it and laid it down on her own terms. It's been eight months since she's used it—her choice, not ours. Still, she's a social butterfly who wants to stay connected with her friends. I get that. Now that she's in high school, she wants her own phone. We had one at home void of bells and whistles, a dumbphone with no Internet or apps ability.

She jumped at the chance to use it and began texting her friends like Morse code, the old-fashioned way, clicking each number two or three times to punch in the next letter. When she came home from school this week, she announced: "Okay, I'm officially a dork."

"How come?"

"Today in social studies, Coach Wilson [her teacher] asked me, 'Grace, why did you bring a garage door opener with you to school today?'"

Boundaries

When a phone becomes your child's newest appendage, it needs a time-out. No one talks on one anyway; it's a high-priced texting machine and compact laptop. Mean mom Kristine Moul shared her family's experience with me: "Mackenzy is fourteen, and we got her an iPhone for her thirteenth birthday. We sat down together and created phone rules. She agreed to *all of them* because she wanted the phone so badly. When we have to take it away, the rules come in handy."

1. This is our phone. We allow you to use it. As long as we are paying the bill and my name is on the contract, you must follow the rules.
2. You are on our iTunes account with our credit card; therefore, you will not download any apps, *even free ones*, without parental permission.
3. We have the right to look at your phone at any time.
4. We reserve the right to take the phone away at any time for any duration of time. Reasons may include: poor grades, bad attitude, lying and misuse of phone.
5. You are not to take the protective cover off the phone ever.

What a great idea—to create the boundaries together.

We Set the Standard

Allison is a mom of three kids and openly admits her addiction to her iPhone. She takes it with her everywhere. I asked her about it. "Yeah, I admit it. I'm addicted." She laughed. "I even sleep with it. I couldn't go a day without it."

Angry Birds, texting, Tweeting, Instagram, and Facebook fill her time. So much so that her husband was ready to toss it *and* their marriage in the wastebasket. "He doesn't like me to be on the phone," she whispered. "He thinks it's a problem."

I reminded her, "You just admitted it was."

"Yeah, but I mean *a real problem*, like drugs are a problem."

This was the model her kids were seeing. She was tossing her marriage to the curb for the next high score on Words with Friends. The following Thanksgiving dinner, her whole family had smartphones parked beside their utensils.

We can't expect our kids to behave differently than we do.

Smartphones Affect Our Parenting, Too

Research shows that face-to-face interaction is important in a child's development. Eating around the table used to be the holy grail of this behavior. When I'm distracted by my phone, I not only lose interest in interaction, I don't respond well as a mom, either.

A new study published in the journal <u>Pediatrics</u> found that adults absorbed in their mobile devices were more likely to harshly scold their children's behavior.

Researchers from Boston Medical Center observed parents interacting with their children during meals in fast food restaurants. They noted that one-third of the adults used their phones continuously during the meals, and 73 percent of them checked their devices at least once.

When a parent who was glued to the phone was interrupted by a child, the parent was apt to react negatively, according to the study. One mother even kicked her child under the table after the child attempted to get her attention while she tapped away at her smartphone. Another mother ignored her child as he tried to lift her head from looking down at a tablet. Researchers believed the kids may have been acting out as a way to test limits or gain the parent's attention.[3]

It's true. If I'm focused on my laptop or smartphone, I can become annoyed pretty quickly. I admit, after researching this topic, I'm seriously thinking about getting rid of my smartphone altogether. Country singers Joey and Rory Feek are from my neck of the woods, and while writing this chapter, I read what they recently did about their smartphones.

Steve Jobs single-handedly gave us the tools we needed to build a successful music career from home, our own unique way. But all that has come with a cost. A heavy cost. Although, we still don't have hi-speed internet at our farm, our iPhones have kept us connected to everyone and everything *at all times*. Our iPhones made it easy to check email, text, tweet, get the weather, watch videos, listen to music, etc . . . but they made it *extremely hard* to focus. Which made it almost impossible to be completely present and in the moment. Joey and I found ourselves checking our emails every 15 minutes, googling our every thought, and texting instead of talking with people. Instead of simplifying our lives, they brought chaos, anxiety and an unhealthy fear that we might miss something.[4]

These two country crooners go on to share how they broke up with their smartphones and are in a good old-fashioned relationship with their flip phones today. After five months, they haven't looked back.

The world's moving forward so fast. Sometimes the only way to slow down is to grab the brake and do something radical, like get rid of your smart phone. What is there to lose? Not much compared to what we gained—the chance to truly *be* with our families, the opportunity to really talk to people again, the chance to be still and hear what God is trying to say to us. Joey and I want to connect less with the things of this world and more with Him. I want to be a better husband and father more than I want to be a better business man or songwriter or artist.[5]

And who wouldn't agree with that?

Mom to Mom

How do you wrestle with technology in your home?

Your children are smarter than you are when it comes to technology. It's a given. Don't ever underestimate your cherub. If you want to see where they've been on the computer, learn how to follow their trails. There isn't enough *babysitting* technology out there to outwit your ever-learning, ever-changing, ever-morphing child.
—**KATIE CHANEY**

The Internet was never meant to be a toy for children, but we parents choose to allow them full access, more often than not. The enemy seeks to kill, steal, and destroy (John 10:10). Never underestimate the enemy and his ability to worm his way into innocent minds. I have seen pastors' reputations destroyed, godly families devastated, and young people's lives captivated by evils of technology. —**MICHELLE BUSCHINI**

At eight, nine, and eleven, our kids don't have phones. I'm surprised at the number of their friends who do—and smartphones to boot. It seems our society has become dependent on the cell phone. It is considered a need, when really it's really a luxury item. —**SARA MUNDAY**

I'm nearly forty-eight and only recently got a smartphone. Might I add I'm not any smarter because of it?
—**ELAINE OLSEN**

I love technology. It's the perfect carrot for homeschool and if chores aren't done. We set guidelines and discuss how cookies get put on your computer, and how you will see these pictures forever. How people can see your history and what you look at, plus this is the pathway for virus invasion on the computer. We especially hit the spiritual aspect of certain pictures and compare it to a stronghold worse than drugs and alcohol. —BECKY PLOTNER

Our daughter has been very responsible with her phone. There are drawbacks, too. The social media aspect must be carefully monitored. Sometimes I take her phone not as a punishment but to give her a break from the texting, etc. With Verizon, I set it up so her phone doesn't receive texts, emails, calls, or FaceTime from 9:30 P.M to 6:30 A.M. Most cell companies have parent controls online; you just have to set them up.
—KRISTINE MOUL

Our kids are eleven, twelve, and fourteen. They all have phones. No smartphones though, only talk and text.
—ANN GOADE

My daughter (age eleven) has a cell phone, not a smartphone. It helps when she's at school because I have on occasion forgotten about some of her after-school activities. She's been asking for a smartphone, but we told her she can get one when she can pay the monthly fees that come with owning a smartphone. I'm hoping that won't be until she's over eighteen (if we're lucky).
—CHERYL CASPER

I admit, we bought our daughter an iPod before she was two; it was for apps and books for when we travelled. She is now four, and I can honestly say she has benefited

from lots of learning apps vs. just watching movies.
—CARMEN SUTHEIMER

℮My daughter is ten and began begging for a phone last year, because all her friends had one. So, we told her when she could afford it, she could have one. Immediately she began finding ways to get one. Extra chores, etc., and she even posted signs around the neighborhood to start her own dog-walking service. I admit, I was nervous because if she was able to buy the phone with the money she made, and afford the whopping monthly service charge, then my sly plan was about to backfire. But the whole idea lost its luster after a while, and we were firm in our non-cell phone efforts.
—JENNY SULPIZIO

℮Our most valuable and effective tools we use to protect our son with technology use have been prayer, open communication, grace in his learning process, and boundaries. —XOCHI DIXON

℮My kiddos are too young, in my opinion (six and eleven) to have a phone, but that doesn't mean we haven't had conversations. They have many school mates, younger than my eleven-year-old, who have them. Entitlement has come to play a little here—*since so-and-so has one and is younger than us, why can't we have one? —*JENNA MARTUCCI

℮Our boys earn screen time through chores. I have a mug of fifteen Popsicle sticks with quick chores on them. They can choose what they want to do and when they're done, they get fifteen minutes of screen time for each chore completed. —ADELLE GABRIELSON

ᴇ⌒While listening to Christian music on YouTube, an ad for an extremely violent video game popped up prior to the music video. I have everything password protected, but I learned a valuable lesson; I can't protect my kids from everything that pops up. —JAMIE JEROME

ᴇ⌒Technology is a necessary tool in our house since we homeschool. We use Family Safety, K9, and family safety routers to filter as best we can. We have timers on our computers to ensure temptation is removed after hours. Computers or electronic devices aren't in bedrooms (so no laptops for us). My oldest is fourteen and does not have a cell phone. However, the most valuable thing we do is talk to our kids about choices, temptations, lies from the enemy, dangers of the Internet, and then allow open discussion about anything they've experienced.

—KIM ANDREWS

Notes

[1] "Generation M2: Media in the Lives of 8- to 18-Year-Olds," Henry J. Kaiser Family Foundation, January 20, 2010, http://kff.org/other/event /generation-m2-media-in-the-lives-of.

[2] Aric Sigman, quoted in Victoria Ward, "Children Using Internet from Age of Three, Study Finds," *Telegraph*, May 1, 2013, www.telegraph.co.uk /technology/internet/10029180/Children-using-internet-from-age-of-three -study-finds.html.

[3] Philip Ross, "Cell Phone Addiction: Parents Glued to Smartphones Have 'More Negative' Interactions with Their Kids," *International Business Times*, March 10, 2014, www.ibtimes.com/cell-phone-addiction-parents-glued -smartphones-have-more-negative-interactions-their-kids-1560588.

[4] Rory Feek, "Flip Phone 5s," *This Life I Live* (blog), April 10, 2014, http:// thislifeilive.com/flip-phone-5s.

[5] Ibid.

PART FOUR

Mean Moms and Motrin

CHAPTER SIXTEEN

Mean Moms Talk Purity

----

*You need to see yourself as a protector of your child's innocence,
guardian of his purity and gatekeeper to his soul.*
—**Dennis Rainey and Barbara Rainey**

Dozens of books have been written on the topic of godly purity.
While I understand a few pages won't come close to doing
this holy attribute justice, it can't be overlooked. A mean
mom is never more befitting of her title than when she tells her
child *no* you can't watch that, *no* you can't leave the house wearing
that, *no* it's not okay to behave like that or talk like that.

Many things fall under the umbrella of purity. In Titus 2, the
older women are encouraged to teach the younger women six
things, and one of them is purity. That's how important this subject is to God.

So I decided to rally the troops. Lots of women came to the
rescue—my ever-faithful Mean Mom Team *plus* a few friends from
The Mom Initiative (Moms on a Mission to Mentor Other Moms),
a ministry I belong to and am passionate about. What I would've
given for a mom to come alongside me when I started mothering.

All of the mean moms you're about to hear from in this chapter model godly parenting from a transparent and real vantage point of "I've been there" and "Let me show you what I've learned."

Angela Mackey

Sex sells. Everything from shampoo and deodorant to lawn mowers. According to a report by Harris Interactive in 2007, 68 percent of TV shows have explicit sexual content.

Listening to degrading sexual lyrics has been shown to speed sexual activity.

Girls with a heavy sexual media diet engage in sexual activity younger than their peers.

Sixty-eight percent of TV shows have explicit sexual content, but only 15 percent of that 68 percent discuss risk and responsibility.[1]

All of the mean moms you're about to hear from in this chapter model godly parenting from a transparent and real vantage point of "I've been there" and "Let me show you what I've learned."

The "wardrobe malfunction" of the 2004 Super Bowl halftime show reminds us even sporting events aren't safe. In a world where our young girls are being sexualized (see *Toddlers and Tiaras*), it's unreasonable to think one sex talk is enough to combat what our culture throws at our kids daily.

Begin an open dialogue about sex with your children at a young age. Then continue the dialogue in age-appropriate ways throughout their lives. Remember sex isn't something dirty or embarrassing. Sex is wonderful when kept in the confines of marriage. God created it. He has a few loving boundaries, not to keep us from enjoying it, but to enjoy it to the fullest.

One final word, friends. We ask you—*urge* is more like it—that you keep on doing what we told you to do to please God, not in a dogged religious plod, but in a living, spirited dance. You know the guidelines we laid out for you from the Master Jesus. God wants you to live a pure life. Keep yourselves from sexual promiscuity. Learn to appreciate and give dignity to your body, not abusing it, as is so common among those who know nothing of God. (1 Thess. 4:1–5 *The Message*)

The vast majority of you are probably thinking, *I was never taught how to do this.* Or, *I messed up, so how can I teach my kids? I don't even know what God says about sex. I am embarrassed.*

Some moms feel like hypocrites teaching purity and abstinence when their own past says otherwise. This should never stop us from sharing what God says is right. Who hasn't lied? Yet, we teach our kids to be honest. Who hasn't stolen something? Yet, we teach our kids not to steal. —JOANNE KRAFT

I faced lots of the same concerns. The alternative is stark though, moms. According to an American Academy of Pediatrics report from 2010, teens acknowledge that media is one of the primary sources for their information about sex.[2] Media—the place where sex without consequences is preached.

Here's the good news. There are many wonderful resources to help you talk to your children about sex.

- *God's Design for Sex.* A series of four books for four different ages. The first book is *The Story of Me,* geared toward three- through five-year-olds. It's age-appropriate and a great way to open the discussion of where babies come from. Each book builds on the information of the previous book and discusses sex, gender, and much more from a biblical perspective.

- *Passport2Purity*. A resource from Family Life Ministries, for children nearing puberty. Used over the course of a weekend away with your child, it's filled with fabulous information and opens up dialogue about when to date and how to protect your purity. They think of everything from hands-on visuals to help your kids understand what God says about sex to ideas that implement an understanding of purity alongside special experiences that weekend with your child.

Finally, remember your children probably know more about sex than you realize. The more you communicate, the more opportunity for a healthy exchange of information. It may be a bit uncomfortable at first, but the results are invaluable.

> Let no one despise your youth, but be an example to the believers in word, in conduct, in love, in spirit, in faith, in *purity*. (1 Tim. 4:12 NKJV; italics added)

Melissa Mashburn

> Pray in the Spirit at all times and on every occasion. Stay *alert* and be *persistent* in your prayers for all believers everywhere. (Eph. 6:18 NLT; italics added)

The teenage years are a wild ride. Buckle up! Remember all those bumps and bruises you went through in their baby, child, and adolescent years? They prepare you for the adventure of parenting your teenager. I'm not trying to scare you, just speaking the truth in love from one mom to another.

Stay Alert
- Be aware of what's going on in your child's life.
- Ask questions, then listen (really listen) when they share things with you.
- Stay involved in their relationships and education.
- Stay connected to their friends and teachers.

Be Persistent
- Never, ever stop praying for your child—they need your prayers now more than ever.
- Though they might resist at first, wait patiently for them to invite you into their world.
- Set up a family dinner night so everyone can talk openly about issues, struggles, and concerns.
- Pray for wisdom in your parenting, yes, even for setting a curfew.

Flee the evil desires of youth and pursue righteousness, faith, love and peace, along with those who call on the Lord out of a pure heart. —2 TIMOTHY 2:22

Julie Sanders

Communication Wisdom from Proverbs
Children still need to listen to their parents' teaching.
(Prov. 1:8)

Children tend to forget what they've heard. (Prov. 3:1)

Children need to attend to a parent's instruction to gain insight. (Prov. 4:1)

Children who accept what they hear will have blessed lives. (Prov. 4:10)

Children who listen are wise. (Prov. 13:1)

Children who stop listening stray. (Prov. 19:27)

God listens to those who seek him. (Prov. 15:29)

Tara Dovenbarger

Among you there must not be even a hint of sexual immorality, or any kind of impurity, or of greed, because these are improper for God's holy people. (Eph. 5:3)

"Mom, is it even possible for me to grow up being sexually pure?" This was the question my thirteen-year-old asked that stopped me in my tracks. I was reminded of the real battle each of our sons and daughters has every day. The bombardment of sexually explicit TV, magazines and billboards along the roads, and relentless commercials and music videos flashing sensuality—and the constant drumming of sex on the Internet—how do we help them navigate through all of this?

Talk, talk, and more talk. They need to know the truth about sexuality. We need to be the ones they feel comfortable to come to with their questions. Be ready with biblically grounded answers. Purity begins with dialogue. Begin by communicating about what they see on TV or in a magazine. Are the bodies real or airbrushed? Why are they dressed that way? What attention are they seeking? Why don't we watch that show? What values do they teach, good or bad?

We aren't victims of some vast conspiracy to ensnare us sexually—we've simply chosen to mix in our own standards of sexual conduct with God's standard. Since we've found God's standard too difficult, we created a mixture—something new, something comfortable, something mediocre. —STEPHEN ARTERBURN AND FRED STOEKER

Teach your children God created sex for us and what he made is good. Joshua Harris writes, "When we embrace our sexuality and claim it for holiness, we are true to who God made us to be. He made us to be holy. In holiness we find the best and ultimately most deeply satisfying expression of our sexuality. And in holiness we experience the truth of what God made. And what God made is good."[3] Encourage your child that sex is most satisfying through God's design in marriage.

Discuss Scripture. King Solomon taught his own son about purity and sexual immorality when he warns of the seductress in Proverbs 5:

> My son, pay attention to my wisdom; lend your ear to my understanding, that you may preserve discretion, and your lips may keep knowledge. For the lips of an immoral woman drip honey, and her mouth is smoother than oil; but in the end she is bitter as wormwood, sharp as a two-edged sword. Her feet go down to death, her steps lay hold of hell. (Prov. 5:1–5 NKJV)

Give real-life examples of how the truth in Scripture plays out. We live in a society that claims there are no consequences to sexual sin, and our kids need to be taught the truth—there are consequences.

Fill them with good things. I'm a firm believer that we should encourage kids to read wholesome, God-honoring books about this topic. We need to not only pray but point them to wisdom. Here are a few books being read by teenagers in our home: *Thoughts for Young Men* by J. C. Ryle and *Sex Is Not the Problem (Lust Is)* by Joshua Harris.

Educate your kids about the opposite sex. Teach them how to treat one another with respect and dignity. Remind them to dress modestly. It's important to teach our girls the struggles some men have with sexual images and purity. Our daughters need to know the truth about the role they play with the men around them.

Model purity. What about you? Are you dressing to look nice— or to seek attention? What are you entertained with that's on TV or the movies? Are you being the example your children need?

So, to answer my son's question, "Yes, you can grow up to be sexually pure. With our God and through his grace, nothing is impossible."

What Mean Moms Have to Say

Katie Chaney: I told my boys, "You can't date until you're forty." *They didn't adhere to that.* But they did have to be sixteen before they even thought about it. In a world full of testosterone-driven males and their drama queen counterparts, we have to be on our guard. But to just say *no* isn't enough. We need to educate the kids— not the schools. I was both embarrassed and empowered when I had *the talk* with my boys. I expressed God's plan for sex and his desire for purity. I explained their role in keeping a young lady pure and asked them, "Would you want someone to be reckless dating your future wife?" I highly recommend swallowing that *awkward feeling* and having *the talk* with them. I'm really glad I did.

Lisa Mattox: I was raised in a Christian home, but my mom's only advice was, "I may not know what you're doing, but God does."

Well, let me tell you . . . that didn't make an iota of a difference when sitting alone in a car with some good-looking young fella. My husband was raised in a non-Christian home. His mom's advice was, "Don't let me catch you doing it in this house!" Needless to say, we're using whatever resources we can find to raise our boys differently.

Susan Basham: We imposed a "no dating until sixteen" rule. As it turned out, our two older kids really didn't date until they were juniors or seniors and then not much. They were picky. Yay! We enforced a strict curfew, and if they blew it, they lost their car keys for a week—which meant they were driven to school by their mom. My experience has been if you shelter kids too much, it backfires. All to say, once you've *trained up a child* and they're ready to fly, you have to let them fly.

Kristine Rasor: My parents failed in this area. I was never taught about God's idea of purity and sex and never told I was beautiful. So, in turn, I looked to other places to have that empty place in my heart filled—when it needed to be filled by God. I teach my daughter she's beautiful on the inside and the outside! We don't have Barbies in our home. I want to teach her even at the age of seven the message of modesty and how certain clothes sexualize women. Dating with a purpose. That's what we plan on teaching our kids.

Katie Chaney: I told my boys, "You can't date until you're forty." They didn't adhere to that. But they did have to be sixteen before they even thought about it. In a world full of testosterone-driven males and their drama queen counterparts, we have to be on our guard. But to just say no isn't enough.

Jessica Fall: My guys are little (three and five). We do not let them have *girlfriends*, even if it is innocent and cute. All of their friends are just that, friends. Right now, we focus on teaching our boys to treat their friends with care and respect, valuing everyone. As far as purity goes, I didn't hear a lot growing up other than *don't do it*. It was our church youth group that really reinforced the *why*. The one thing I found frustrating as a teen was when I was told to *guard my heart*—what did they mean? Now I get it, there are consequences when you share the deeper places of your heart with others. Emotional intimacy is to be guarded as much as physical intimacy. I will teach my boys the importance of having good boundaries around their heart and saving those deeper places for a treasured relationship.

Rachael McKinney: Purity and sex and the dangers of it all wasn't discussed in my home. I wish it had been. We are very open about it, to an appropriate degree, with our kids (nine and eleven). Dating isn't far away. A verse I've begun to hold on to is 2 Corinthians 10:4–5, about taking every thought captive. I've seen and learned the danger of impurity and how it begins in our thoughts—as they grow, this will be a verse we teach: "For the weapons of our warfare are not carnal but mighty in God for pulling down strongholds, casting down arguments and every high thing that exalts itself against the knowledge of God, bringing every thought into captivity to the obedience of Christ" (NKJV).

Sara Munday: My parents tried their best to teach us about purity. I wasn't allowed to date until I was sixteen, but chose not to until I was seventeen. Everything was great until my college years— then my parents didn't seem to know so much. I pray my failures coupled with my husband's success at purity will help us teach our children. We will talk to them about courting rather than dating— at five years old, my daughter had a boy who was already pledging his undying love and wanted to marry her. At first we thought it was an innocent crush, but somehow this boy knew more than he should, and it became more serious than we thought possible. We've been concerned to discover kids we know between the ages of eight and eleven and how well-versed they are about the dating game—even how to kiss in a romantic way. We've stepped up our game to make sure our children know what is and isn't acceptable at their age. We encourage dating only in pursuit of marriage—in other words, court, not date.

Forty-six percent of high school students in the US have had sexual intercourse. Although sex is common, most sexually active teens wish they'd waited longer to have sex, which suggests that sex is occurring before youths are prepared for its consequences. One case of an STD is diagnosed for every four sexually active teens.[4]

Thanks for the help, ladies. Paul and I believe purity is taught in the home first. Last year, I used Family Life Ministry's *Passport2Purity* program and took Grace to a hotel for the weekend to watch their DVDs and spend some quality girl time together. My husband took our oldest son, David, away and used *Passport2Purity* as his guide a few years before. I highly recommend this personal purity conference for two—mom and daughter or father and son.

When I did a little research, I discovered that thirty-seven states teach abstinence in this country. I'm grateful to be living in one of them. Still, the number of pregnancies and STDs are staggering. Being a Christian parent doesn't mean I sit around all day and pray my child will do the right thing. I teach my children about contraceptives and contractual disease, too. Why? For the same reason I teach my children about drugs and alcohol: not so they'll partake, but so they'll be knowledgeable.

Most importantly, we encourage our four children to know and understand what God says about marriage and sex, and we seek continual resources to reinforce Biblical purity. We hold our children to a high standard and don't shrink back when our culture says differently.

Mom to Mom

What do you teach your kids about purity?

No dating, just friendships until marrying age. There's no reason to date unless you're looking for a spouse. My daughter and I have been to purity events to encourage what I do at home. —CATHY SIMPKINS

Dating is for finding your partner in life, not just to have someone to hang out with. —ERIKA HRANICKY

We're not big fans of dating as a rite of passage. We remind them to "Be the person you want to date one day." We encourage them to focus on *their* growth first. You date for the purpose of marriage. Why would I encourage my child to partake in something painful? Every dating relationship that doesn't end in marriage ends in a broken heart. Why in the world would I want my child to experience that? —CHELSEA MORROW

Notes

[1] Caroline Knorr, "Too Sexy Too Soon," *Common Sense Blog*, Common Sense Media, February 8, 2011, www.commonsensemedia.org/blog/too-sexy -too-soon.

[2] Victor C. Strasburger, "Sexuality, Contraception, and the Media," policy statement, *Pediatrics* 126, no. 3 (2010): 576–582, http://pediatrics. aappublications.org/content/126/3/576.short.

[3] Joshua Harris, *Sex Is Not the Problem (Lust Is)* (Colorado Springs: Multnomah, 2003).

[4] Rebecca L. Collins, Marc N. Elliott, Sandra H. Berry, David E. Kanouse, Dale Kunkel, Sarah B. Hunter, and Angela Miu, "Watching Sex on Television Predicts Adolescent Initiation of Sexual Behavior," *Pediatrics* 114, no. 3 (September 1, 2004): e280–e289, doi: 10.1542/peds. 2003-1065-L.

Mean Moms Drag Kids to Church

Most of us spend the first six days of each week sowing wild oats;
then we go to church on Sunday and pray for a crop failure.
—**Fred Allen**

We never thought this could happen to us, *to our family.*
Our daughter has a drug problem. We've drug her to
church for months now.

The signs are pretty easy to spot. Have you noticed some
changes in behavior? Sunday mornings are usually the worst. Is
your child difficult to rouse out of bed—a little edgy and biting
with her words? Does she shoot angry glances, or use heavy-footed
stomping throughout the house? If so, then you may have a drug
problem in your home, too.

Pastor Chuck Smith, founder of Calvary Chapel Costa
Mesa, loved to share, "When I was young, I had a drug
problem. My mom drug me to church every Sunday!"

You may be one of the lucky ones. Your child is drug-free. He gladly stands beside you each week singing "Amazing Grace" at the top of his lungs and you couldn't be prouder. Unfortunately, not every parent has this experience. On our drive to church, my daughter stares out our van window like a prisoner headed to her incarceration.

In her defense, she used to love attending church. But when her best girlfriend moved away, she was heartbroken. For years we joyously attended together as a family. Then this awful attitude of hers became our unwanted guest. She would sulk and pout until we were all brought into her not-so-happy world of angst and gloom.

When I began to poll my girlfriends, I discovered this drug problem was more common than I'd thought. My girlfriend still attends the traditional church we belonged to as children, where sacraments are often taken as a way of expressing spiritual growth. My journey of faith took me over to the Protestant side of Christianity. We were on the phone when she shared a story. Her son was about to receive his sacrament of confirmation, and she was listening as the priest addressed the crowd of young adults and their parents: "You have a choice to make. I ask that you don't take this sacrament lightly. If you have any doubt in your mind, it would be best if you don't receive this Blessed Sacrament."

"Joanne, as soon as we got in the car, I said, "You, son, have no choice. You *will* be receiving the sacrament of confirmation."

If you knew my unabashedly tolerant, soft-hearted friend, you would've laughed as hard as I did when she shared her words with me about her teenager. This was the hill she would die on. Sounds a lot like a mean mom, doesn't it?

Research Suggests Dragging Works

A national study by the Barna Research Group of Ventura, California, found that roughly seven out of ten Americans adults (71 percent) had a period of time during their childhood when they regularly attended a Christian church. It seems old habits die hard: a majority of those who attended church as a youngster still attend regularly today (61 percent), while a large majority of those who were not churchgoers as children are still absent from churches today (78 percent). Thus adults who were drug to church as children show lifelong effects.[1]

Apparently, dragging kids to church is a universal tug-of-war in homes every Sunday morning. When I asked another friend if she'd ever experienced some Sabbath pullback, she immediately shared. "When my oldest son turned eighteen, he was quite sure he didn't really *have* to go. So I took him aside and had a loving motherly chat with him." My friend smiled with a twinkle in her eye only another mean mom would appreciate.

"Go on," I prodded.

"I told him that I basically paid for his existence. I paid the mortgage, the food he ate, clothing, all of it. He had heat in the winter and air conditioning in the summer. I reminded my son that I went to work every single day to afford these things for him. So, in turn, I didn't ask—I required he honor me by giving an hour and a half of his precious time every week to sit with me in church service."

"I bet that didn't go over well," I laughed.

"I told him it was the very least he could do for me as a thank you." She leaned back in her chair and added, "He asked me, 'How would *you* feel if *your* mom made you go to church when you were eighteen?' And I said simply, 'I wish she had. Perhaps I wouldn't have made the many unsavory mistakes I made in my lifetime. Son, now I know where to look for answers and who to talk to and who to thank.'"

"So, you've got to tell me. Did he go with you to church?"

"He went to church with his brother and me every day since." She smiled.

Mean Mom Intervention

Mean moms don't believe they can force their child to love Jesus. That is a working of the Holy Spirit. Still, attending church together is not an option, so they don't make it one. If these things were up for debate, children would never eat broccoli or string beans, either.

> *Mean moms don't believe they can force their child to love Jesus. That is a working of the Holy Spirit.*

I fought against the childhood fears and voices in my head. *I can't drag my teenager to church. The Bible was shoved down my throat as a child. I don't want to do that to my children.* God's Word silenced them all: *Train her up in the way she should go.*

There was about to be an intervention.

Sitting down with my almost-grown girl, I could see hints of the once hardheaded toddler. "Honey, I know you aren't enjoying church right now. But it's not your choice to make. You live in a household that honors God and attends church as a family. And you are a very special part of this family." Her vacant stare came into focus. "While you live in our home, you will honor your father and me and our decision to attend church."

Mean Mom Update

My daughter is now a grown adult. When she finished high school, she announced she'd be attending a Christian college. After battling so many Sunday mornings, we were a wee bit surprised.

When your child moves out, you discover whether or not God is a priority. No longer was I there to wake her up and prod her along to Sunday service. When she moved four hundred miles away, she could do whatever she wanted. I couldn't drag her anywhere anymore, and I didn't nag her or check up on her, either. She was free to do as she desired on Sundays.

Had I made my child hate going to church while she was in my home? Did she have a relationship with Jesus? Or had I pushed her farther away from him? I wondered.

The phone rang and my girl's sing-song voice said, "Hi, Mom. Guess what? I think I've found my church."

Were these words really coming out of my daughter's mouth? *Don't act too excited, Joanne.* I began a silent checklist that would only frighten her if spoken aloud: *What's the name of the church? Get it. Look it up on the Internet. Read their doctrine of faith. Who is her pastor? Does he have a degree? Does he have a blog? Read it. Does the congregation bring their Bibles on Sunday? Or, is this one of those namby-pamby Jesus-lite fellowships? Above all, remain calm.* I coached myself silently.

"That's wonderful. Tell me about it, sweetheart." I sounded relaxed, like she was sharing her grocery list with me—while I drew blood biting my tongue from the onslaught of questions playing tennis in my head. I underestimated my daughter—she knew me well and answered them all.

"The pastor is really great. He makes the Bible come alive. He teaches from the Word every Sunday, Mom, so bringing our Bibles is a must. And the worship is phenomenal! The worship leader is a graduate from my college. He's great. And you know what? I'm going to volunteer to serve in the children's ministry." She laughed. Was she remembering the years of painful Sunday mornings like I was? This was a *mean mom* payday.

One Thousand Excuses

Church attendance is as vital to a disciple as a transfusion of rich, healthy blood to a sick man. —DWIGHT L. MOODY[2]

When children don't want to go to church, they can come up with a thousand excuses. Do you have children who dislike attending church with you? Have you asked them why? Communicate and allow them to share. You can validate their feelings without validating an excuse. I've listed a few of the common ones below.

Boring. "But, Mom, it's soooooooooooooooo boring." Who hasn't heard that line before? We have a Kraft family tradition on Sunday mornings. On our way home each week, Paul or I will ask, "What did you learn today?" It's fun and sometimes funny to hear their different answers:

- "I learned God knows the exact number of hairs I have on my head."
- "I learned about patience today, and realize you and Dad need more of it."
- "I learned never to sit by Brandon after he's eaten garlic the night before."

When my son said, "I didn't learn anything today," I shared with him, "That's okay, but remember God's Word is supernatural, son. I struggle sometimes, myself, but I heard a great saying, 'If you leave church with absolutely nothing, then maybe you came in too full of yourself.'"

Not every sermon is going to be a spiritual grand slam. But, when God's word is taught, I will walk out with a tiny piece of him, a Scripture, a gentle reminder, or a word of encouragement to help me get through the next week.

Friends. When your kids are little, whether they love church or not has a lot to do with the friends they have there. I remember when we were church shopping years ago, the pastor was phenomenal at teaching God's Word in an easy-to-understand way—my husband and I were sold. Except our kids weren't making friends.

One Sunday, I looked down the pew and saw Grace staring straight ahead, her eyes welling up with tears, and one slowly rolled down her cheek and splashed onto her blouse. She couldn't have planned it any better. Not the kind of experience you want your baby girl to have in church. Paul and I decided to continue our hunt for a church home.

Hypocrisy. "No one can spot a hypocrite faster than a child." I'm not quite sure who said that, but those words have stuck with me. How many adults do you know who no longer attend church because of hypocrisy witnessed in the church when they were young, or even old, for that matter? I remind my kids a church is a hospital for sin-sick people—and we all need spiritual mending.

For me, using the hypocrisy argument for not attending church is a cop-out. I need to keep my eyes on Jesus, not on ministry leaders or fellow church members. Human beings will let me down every time. I cringe to think of my own children and their memories of hypocrisy in me. It's important to teach our kids how much Jesus hated hypocrisy, too. It shouldn't be anyone's reason for not attending church.

I'd like to give you one important tidbit of advice. Don't assume just because something is labeled Christian it is. Do your homework. When you attend a church, make a point to meet your child's Sunday school teacher and youth group leader. Get to know them. I consider myself a spiritual homeschooler, so I believe what my children know about God depends on what I teach them. That's why I make sure whoever is teaching them on Sunday or Wednesday knows God, too.

I remember hearing a woman share once, "Be careful when putting your children in a place to learn a little something about God. Because they may just learn that their God is a little something." As much as I love a glazed donut and a talented worship band, I remind myself that what I draw my children with, I draw them to. If bells and whistles are what I'm using to entice my teenager to worship God on the Sabbath, then, well, I'm doing the Lord a great disservice.

Does your child have a drug problem? You might consider forced rehab for a while. Will I ever apologize for dragging my daughter to church? Never. As a parent, and because I love her, I did the best I could to lead her to Living Water. It was up to her to drink. Thankfully, she did.

Mom to Mom

Do you drag your kids to church?

❧ I'm all for it. I think it's about showing your kids what's important to you—walking the walk, so to speak. You can't model behavior or belief if you sit in the pew and they sit at home. Drag away! —MICHELLE MCDONALD

❧ We drag or push our kids on the bus to go to school, don't we? What is more important to our existence as Christians than taking them to learn about and worship God and the reason why we are here? —LYNN PEPE

❧ Church was never something that was discussed as an option when I was growing up. It was just part of life. I never felt like I was forced. I treated my kids the same way. We just went. It has always just been what we do. —EVA STOCKTON

❧ We didn't force church attendance. We'd invite them to go with us every week, discuss what we learned about later, and talk frequently about what the Lord was doing in our lives and theirs. I know it's not a perfect solution, but I pray often they will continue to desire to grow their own faith, knowing that God will perfect the faith that was begun. —JULIE HICKS

Notes

[1] "Adults Who Attended Church As Children Show Lifelong Effects," Barna Group website, November 5, 2001, www.barna.org/barna-update/5-barna -update/62-adults-who-attended-church-as-children-show-lifelong-effects#. U0MxwPldUmE.

[2] Janet Parshall, "Key to Healthy Living Can Be Found in Church Pews," *Christian Post,* May 6, 2013, www.christianpost.com/news/key-to-healthy -living-can-be-found-in-church-pews-95312.

CHAPTER EIGHTEEN

Mean Moms Eradicate Entitlement

- -

Children with entitlement issues are trained to believe
they are on equal footing with parents and won't care
about your discomfort, only their own.
—**Joanne Kraft**, *Just Too Busy*

A teen girl sued her chief of police father for child support and tuition to continue attending her private school and future college, *after* she reached the legal adult age of eighteen, and *after* she ran away because of house rules she didn't want to keep and chores she didn't want to do.

A North Texas teen from an affluent family made headlines when he was sentenced to probation and rehabilitation after he killed four pedestrians when he lost control of his speeding pickup truck while driving drunk. A psychologist called as an expert defense witness said the boy suffered from *affluenza*.

According to Dr. Ralph Minear, author of *Kids Who Have Too Much*, affluenza—or rich kid syndrome—attacks not only the children of the wealthy but also those in middle-class and low-income families.[1] Giving a child excessive freedom, money, food, information, and protection can bring on this syndrome.

Affluenza, really? I think we need to call it what it is: entitlement.

Entitlement is the belief you have a right to something, when you have no right at all. A right always comes at the expense of someone else, by the way. To simplify it: as a parent, you're giving too much and expecting too little. When I feed a child's every want without any work on their part, I nurture an attitude of entitlement. Kids who believe they are beneficiaries of anything their parents can do for them, without responsibility or acknowledging the true giver, will grow into weak adults who expect rights at others' expense and without gratitude for the right given.

When a child becomes an adult with entitlement issues, a parent is pained by guilt. *Is it my fault my child behaves this way?* Oftentimes, it is. While outside influences, like friends, books, and movies, definitely can encourage entitlement, it's up to me to address and eradicate it. It's the mama bird's responsibility to gently nudge her baby bird out of the nest and teach it to fly. Mama bird will be there when it falls, not to fly it around on her back, but to continue to nudge it out of the nest again and again until baby bird is flying solo.

If my kids expect me to fulfill their wants and needs, dreams and desires, I have failed. —JOANNE KRAFT

Teach the Difference between a Want and a Need

"I need a cell phone," Samuel remarked. A seventh grader in junior high, he needed a lesson on want and need.

"Why?" I asked.

"Everyone has one. I'm the only kid in the world that doesn't have one. Plus, they're cool."

"You *need* air to breathe. You *need* water and food. You don't *need* a phone."

As our culture becomes more affluent, we bestow more and more *stuff* on our children—an outward demonstration of our love, which feeds their appetite for things. It's shortsighted to parent this way. If this is love, we're loving our kids to death.

For where your treasure is, there your heart will be also. (MATT. 6:21 NKJV)

Giving Too Much

Watching my daughter graduate from junior high was a precious time. Meghan was chosen to give the graduation speech for her class. We were so proud. Her father was sent to spy out the land and conquer front-row seats. In 95-degree weather and without any shade, he baked for over an hour before the family arrived to take our place in the audience.

Watching hundreds of thirteen-year-old boys and girls walk across the stage was an eye-opener for me. Young ladies sported full-on prom-like dresses with red-carpet hairstyles and manicures to boot. Later, when I had a chance to talk with my daughter, I asked her, "Meg, I noticed a lot of the girls had professional hair and nails done. They sure went all-out for eighth grade graduation, huh?"

"Oh, Mom, you have no idea. Sarah's mom took her to Nordstrom to buy her graduation dress; Katie's mom took her to have her hair, nails, *and* toes done. And did you see the limo? A couple of families pitched in to have their kids chauffeured to graduation."

What mom doesn't want to pour out a lavish *ta-da* over her son or daughter? I understand the desire. But where do you go from there? Will they ever be happy with a homemade cake and one close friend for their birthday? More, bigger, better becomes the mantra. Maybe for high school graduation they could be shot like cannon into their new car, bought on your dime, of course. We all love our children passionately. But beware of overdoing it. Just because you can afford to do something extravagant doesn't always mean you should.

Never love kids with stuff. When we bestow material items and advantages, we steal character-building opportunities to model responsibility and thankfulness. —JOANNE KRAFT

Extreme Birthday Parties

Grace ran in, waving the birthday invitation in the air. "Mom, look. Eva is having a birthday party and I'm invited." She was nine years old, and I understood what a big deal this was to her.

"That's great, honey." I gave her a big hug.

Placing the invitation on the kitchen counter, Grace scampered off to another part of the house to share the news with her brother Samuel.

Picking up the invite, I began to read. The festivities would begin at a water park with a barbecue, followed by a slumber party and next-day fun. Pick-up time was the late afternoon. A twenty-four-hour birthday party for a nine-year-old? Water park, barbecue, *and* slumber party? That seemed a bit much to me. *But it's not any of my business*, I thought to myself.

Meghan was once invited to a birthday party where the girls were all picked up in a limousine, then driven to the mall for pedicures, with a pit stop at their favorite burger joint, before heading back home. I remember wondering, *Who is this little girl, a foreign dignitary?*

Now, before you wonder if I live in Beverly Hills, think again. We lived in a suburban neighborhood in the foothills of the Sierra Nevada Mountains at the time. Average middle-class families with parents who worked hard for what they had. Their greatest struggle? The same one we all have. Telling their kids "no."

Responsibility—Get Creative

How do you extinguish entitlement in your kids?
Expect more from them—and the sooner the better.

When is it time to give them jobs around the house? I promise it's earlier than you think. Revisit my chapter on hard work and chores if you're still unsure. Each day we have a chance to teach our kids about responsibility and, in the process, gratefulness.

When our children were between the ages of three and thirteen, we surprised them with a trip to Disneyland. There was just one problem. We'd saved enough money to purchase the admission tickets, but we didn't have money for snacks or souvenirs inside the park.

When we addressed this with our kids, we came up with a solution: a garage sale and lemonade stand. It didn't take a rocket scientist to see our garage was bulging at the seams. My husband and I went into the garage with our kids to sort through boxes and stacks of items collected over the years.

While our nine-year-old and twelve-year-old helped gather items throughout the house, our three-year-old and five-year-old helped me make lemonade and dozens of cookies. All four of our children helped create colorful garage sale signs, and a few "Help us get to Disneyland" flyers were passed out to advertise the date and time to members of our church and around the neighborhood.

Entitlement is self-centered selfishness on steroids. —JOANNE KRAFT

The lemonade stand was up and running at 6 A.M. on the day of our big garage sale. Lots of people showed up to support their hard work. People respect and encourage kids who try hard. Could it be because they don't see it enough? The kids ended up earning over $275. After deducting the money spent to make lemonade and cookies, divided by four, they each received $65 to spend inside the park, more than enough to purchase Mickey Mouse ears and a couple of churros while we were there.

While on this trip, I remember stopping for a meal. We ordered the family breakfast special, and our daughter wanted an orange juice. "That adds another $2 to our total. We'll buy everyone something to eat and drink, but if you want the juice, you'll have to pay the difference." Guess who decided against orange juice?

Teaching children the value of hard work and responsibility helps them understand finances and the difference between a want and a need. Once they earn money themselves, it's eye-opening how they finally understand how hard their parents work for wants and needs, too. When our teens want or need a new pair of shoes, we pay a set amount. If our children want something bigger, better, or with a flashy swoosh on the side, they need to pitch in to pay the difference. Kids need to have some skin in the game.

This only works if you encourage your teenager to work for cash in some way. Our son is thirteen, and he just began an after-school job to help at a farm nearby. He's paid a little bit each day he shows up to clean out stalls and milk calves. When Grace and Samuel began refereeing soccer games last year, they were twelve and fourteen, respectively. It was their first taste of working for money. Grace has gone on to do weekly babysitting for families in our neighborhood. She was quite resourceful and went door-to-door with a flyer, meeting new parents and handing them her business card. I just loved the tagline beneath her name: "...because every child needs a little grace."

We make a point to instill a solid work ethic in our children. Telling children to work will never be successful. Working and bringing them alongside you has a much greater effect. Recently, we needed to paint the inside of our garage. In ninety-degree weather, no one was looking forward to it. But we grabbed some ice water, threw on our grubby clothes, and tackled that job as a team. Were our teens thrilled to be helping? Not at first. Were they excited to work alongside us for nothing more than ice water and pepperoni pizza? Not especially. But the finished product looks great, and our kids gained a few bragging rights to share with their kids one day.

Years ago, when my husband was in between law school and passing the bar, we were going through some financial hardships, and he took a job throwing a newspaper. Our oldest two were young enough to go along with their daddy on the weekends to help him throw the paper. He offered to pay them in chocolate donuts—what kid wouldn't love that deal?

One warning, though: do not reward every single thing your child does with money or food, or anything else. Sometimes saying, "Thank you. I appreciate how much you helped today," needs to be enough.

Entitlement and gratefulness cannot coexist. These two attitudes are mutually exclusive. Like a magnet deflects iron, entitlement deflects gratefulness. —JOANNE KRAFT

Cars and College Tuition Are Not a Right

"Sophia got a car for her sixteenth birthday!" our kids announced. We didn't buy the kids cars, nor pay for their insurance or gas either. We didn't buy them cell phones or smartphones, and they somehow managed to survive this modern-day child abuse.

Did they always appreciate our training? Nope. But my daughter graduated college in three years, and my son is working toward becoming a veterinarian. If he succeeds, he'll be the first doctor in our family. My kids are smart but no smarter than anyone else; the edge they have over their generation is we taught them they can accomplish much through hard work.

As a parent, the time will come when you'll have to make some tough choices about what you will or won't pay for. One friend shared, "We have two kids so we can pay for their college years." Her kids go to four-year colleges and are getting good grades. Plus, they thank her: a good sign she raised kids who aren't entitled.

College tuition is not a right. Depending on the state you live in, annual college tuition can run anywhere from five to fifty thousand dollars annually—now multiply that times four. Using retirement money to support your children's future isn't smart, especially since they have a much longer time to pay back a college loan. Do you have that sort of money saved? If not, you may have to say "no." Here's what financial guru Dave Ramsey has to say about it:

> As tough as it may be to focus on your own retirement security rather than provide a paid-for college education for your kids, you're actually doing your kids a favor.
>
> If you deplete your retirement savings, or if you don't save for retirement at all because you put all your money towards college, you could end up depending on your kids instead of supporting yourself during retirement.

You have tons of options to pay for college: scholarships, grants, part-time jobs, work study . . . anything but student loans! But when it comes to retirement, your savings is all you have to rely on. Choosing your retirement over your kids' college doesn't make you a bad parent; it makes you a responsible parent.[2]

Adding entitlement to the mix, you could have a young adult who plays harder than he studies. Paying for your college student to party for four years on your dime while bringing home subpar grades creates a situation that warrants a remedy. Just because you can afford to send your children to school doesn't mean they have the right to waste that opportunity.

Eradicate Entitlement—Teach Gratitude

> Gratitude is the attitude that sets the altitude for living. —JAMES MACDONALD

Would you like to kill an entitlement attitude? Teach a little gratitude. Does your child watch or hear you being thankful? Are you kind with your words? How do you treat someone who serves you in a restaurant? Serving others less fortunate is a beautiful way to teach gratitude. Here are a few others:

- *Neighborhood*—Single moms, widows, families in need are all around us if we'd just look. Choose a family to serve each month. Mow a lawn, rake leaves, shovel snow, drop off a bag of groceries, or offer free babysitting for an evening.

- *Retirement homes*—Bring flowers to someone who doesn't receive visitors. The attendant at the front desk will be more than happy to point you to an elderly person in need of company.
- *Caregivers*—So many people are caring for the sick in their own homes. Confined to care, they don't have opportunities for refreshment. Offer to sit with their loved one for a few hours while they take a much-needed break.
- *Make a meal*—Get busy in the kitchen and drop off a meal for a sick or needy family or a home in your neighborhood that just welcomed a new baby. If you can't think of one, pray together and ask the Lord to bring one to mind.

> *Mean moms understand they're working themselves out of a job. That doesn't mean love ends. When you teach them to stand on their own, it is successful parenting.*

A fantastic gratitude exercise is saying grace as a family. Don't wait for dinnertime to express your heartfelt thanks to a loving God. Breakfast and lunch are wonderful opportunities, too.

With six of us in our family, early on I decided to assign each child a day of the week to lead us in grace. Not only has it been exceptionally sweet to hear them thank God for my meatloaf, it's taught them to be thankful. Plus, the additional benefit? Corporate prayer is not feared.

Keep in mind, mean moms don't do what their children can do for themselves. When my adult kids share stories today, you'd think they worked the coal mines. Still, they've earned respect from their peers, gained self-esteem that can't be taught in a book, and ultimately attained independence. Mean moms understand they're working themselves out of a job. That doesn't mean love ends. When you teach them to stand on their own, it is successful parenting.

The greatest compliment I can get is not that my kids need me, but that they don't.

Scrooged is a favorite Christmas movie of ours. Bill Murray plays the role of a modern-day Scrooge with sarcastic wit that has us laughing every year. He delivers our favorite line with condescending grace: "Sometimes I give so much it hurts. I have to tell myself stop." In theory, parents exist to sacrifice and pour out their lives: giving until it hurts is applauded. It's crazy to encourage moms to give less, but in our American culture today, it's what we need to do.

We need to see giving differently. We need to give less of what they want and shine a spotlight on their true need—lessons in fiscal and personal responsibility with a double helping of gratefulness.

Mom to Mom

What do mean moms have to say about entitlement and keeping up with the Joneses?

More and more parents are afraid to hurt their children's self-esteem or their children will not have everything their friends have. As a society we've allowed the *keeping up with the Joneses* to trickle down to our children. We're no longer giving the children an opportunity to learn from failing. We swoop in to make everything better. We try to buy our children's affection rather than spending time with them. —SARA MUNDAY

We do children a huge disservice playing into an entitlement attitude and ignoring our God-given positions. —MICHELLE BUSCHINI

I'm a *meanish* mom and getting meaner as my kids get older. I definitely don't want to send them out into the world entitled and incapable. When perceived rights become a bigger focus than true responsibilities, it can get pretty ugly. Entitlement is a dreadful thing. The fruit of entitlement can be seen in the actions of a spoiled child . . . throwing a temper tantrum because she doesn't get what she wants when she wants it with no thought of others. Unfortunately, the very good we hope to do by giving handouts can lead to a great fall that cannot maintain a culture of personal responsibility. It's true with our kids. It's true with our country. —TEASI CANNON

I think this generation's biggest problem is thinking we need to give our children what we never had. It's crazy. Today, parents give less responsibilities and less work. It has led people to think things should be given to them. It's sheer laziness. A mean mom has her children do housework, help the family meet its needs even if that means getting a job to help contribute. Not allowing materialism to influence her children by buying them only the best. —JACQUE LEDFORD

Notes

[1] Ralph E. Minear and William Proctor, *Kids Who Have Too Much* (Nashville: Thomas Nelson, 1989).

[2] Dave Ramsey, *The Total Money Makeover: A Proven Plan for Financial Fitness* (Nashville: Thomas Nelson, 2003).

CHAPTER NINETEEN

Mean Moms Friend Their Teens

All I know is that I carried you for nine months. I fed you,
I clothed you, I paid for your college education. Friending me
on Facebook seems like a small thing to ask in return.

—Jodi Picoult

If Facebook were a country, it would be the third most populated in the world. At 1.3 billion users to date, it surpasses the number of people in both the United States and Russia combined—three times.

If Facebook were my boyfriend, we would be the quintessential high school couple—I've broken up with Facebook more times than I can count. I'm back for now and wondering daily, *Why are we still together?* Or better yet, *Why am I looking at Darrin and Kristen's honeymoon pictures from Niagara Falls? I don't even know Darrin and Kristen.*

Facebook is being used by everyone from the Fortune 500 businessman to farmers in third-world countries. There's no denying that it's a fantastic connection tool. I polled my own followers on Facebook and asked, "Why do you use Facebook?" The one common denominator they all expressed? To keep in touch with family and friends.

With the majority of the American population with a personal profile on this social network, we need to learn how to navigate these tricky waters with our teenagers. Facebook is just an example. It's not a favorite for kids anymore. Why? Because too many of their parents are there now, so teens have migrated to social networking sites like Instagram, Twitter, and, my least favorite, Snapchat. For now, since most of us moms understand Facebook, it's a good place to begin.

How do we teach great kids that something meant for good can also be used to distract our attentions and destroy reputations? Because even great kids make mistakes. You'd be surprised how many parents have dialed 9-1-1 for their social media answers.

My phone line lit up and I mentally prepared for the next emergency. *Is it a vehicle accident? Maybe a domestic violence call? Lord, I don't want another suicidal caller tonight; those are so tough.* It only took a few seconds to recognize that the male voice on the other end didn't have a life-or-death emergency to report—but I couldn't have told him otherwise.

"9-1-1 Emergency."

"I need your help."

"What's your emergency?"

"My wife and I don't know what to do. We recently discovered our teenage daughter is using Facebook inappropriately. We've tried to get in touch with Facebook through their website, but no one is getting back to us."

"Sir, is she using her page for criminal activity?"

"Well, no. . . ."

"Then the police department has no legal jurisdiction."

"What do we do?" It was clear he was discouraged. I felt bad for him. God knew I was going to answer the phone when he called, so I decided to be quite frank.

"If she were my daughter, I'd have her delete her account, or if she won't do that, I guess I'd have to delete it myself."

"That's the problem. She won't delete it and she won't give us her password. We don't know what to do, and apparently we're finding out there's nothing we can do."

Okay, moms, this is where I have to stop my story and interject a little *mean mom* truth here. I have a big problem understanding statements like "there's nothing we can do" from parents. If I hadn't been on a recorded line, I would've said, "Remember, you are the parent. She is the child." Whether children are two or twenty-two— if they depend on your financial blessings to survive, they're a child. Don't be discouraged. There are always consequences to any situation. It just depends on how much time and energy a parent is willing to sacrifice.

Okay, back to my story . . .

"Sir, did your teenager purchase that laptop herself? Does she pay for the wireless Internet service that keeps her Facebook account active in your home? Does she have her own car or does she drive yours? Does she enjoy the freedom of hanging out with her girlfriends? Does she have a cell phone?"

"I see what you're saying."

"I understand the frustration of raising a teenager and not knowing what to do, but you and your wife hold a lot more cards than you think."

I wish I could say this was the only time I received a call like this. You'd be amazed at how many I've answered over the years.

Blessing or Beast?

In our home, our children don't get a green light for a Facebook account just because their friends have one. I struggle with my child missing out on the social interaction, but my husband makes a compelling argument. While writing this chapter, I asked him to share his thoughts. Our children have been heard to say, "Dad you're the Old Testament, and Mom you're the New Testament." Let's just say he puts me to shame in the boundaries department.

"What do you think are some of the benefits of Facebook or Instagram or Twitter?"

"There aren't any."

"Oh, c'mon, you can't think of one?"

"You can't convince me of the benefits for children. Sure, it's a social thing and I get that. There is a personal benefit to being a part of something all the other kids are a part of. But just because something has a few beneficial qualities doesn't make it good."

"So, you don't think any teenager should have a Facebook page?"

"No, I didn't say that. Here's the thing, Joanne. You'll never convince me soda pop is good for our kids, but that doesn't mean we should ban our kids from drinking soda. Where Facebook is concerned, parents just need to really be on top of it. If they don't understand it, then it shouldn't be handed over to their kids."

If you're in the Facebook-has-no-redeeming-qualities camp, then you might just want to mosey on over to the next chapter. There's isn't anything more for you to see here. Though I must admit, after navigating social networking with our two oldest children, I'm siding with him more and more.

> *It's not technology that's the problem—*
> *it's our misuse of it.* —DR. ARCHIBALD HART

My twenty-three-year-old daughter said, "I'm not a big believer in social media being this awful thing. It really depends on the person. If a teenager is too sensitive and doesn't have much common sense, they probably aren't ready. But, if they're mature and understand how to use it wisely, then I think they should be able to."

Of course, my husband would argue the same is true about soda pop.

I jumped on the Facebook train to have the ability to reach my readers and to keep my finger on the pulse of the fast-changing world of Christian publishing. For me, what began with good intentions quickly evolved into something different. My spare time, once used to garden, write, and work around the house, was quickly filled with incomplete sentences and an insane number of selfies by people I'll never meet. They called to me like a mermaid's siren song, and before long, my daily to-do list was obliterated against the rocks.

I realized spending more time in face-to-face relationships makes more sense to me; coffee dates with friends leave little room for miscommunication. Plus, I noticed I didn't always feel good after seeing people I love on social media participate in language or post photos that were offensive and sadly inappropriate. For me, it hasn't always been a fun ride, and I was inspired by my Aunt Judy recently, who said, "I'm giving up Facebook for Lent." When I checked back with her a few weeks later, she said, "It was hard at first because so many of our family and friends keep in touch there. But, it just isn't my favorite way to stay connected. I enjoy a phone call or a visit more." True to form, my aunt promotes phone calls over text messages, too. She's a great example to me that relationships need to be nurtured the old-fashioned way.

Important for Teens to Know

I feel sorry for this generation. When I was a teenager, I could make a muddled, jumbled mess without much fanfare. Nowadays, with cell phone cameras and instant messaging, kids hold the power to turn a small speed bump of a problem into a mountain of pain and shame in a matter of minutes.

I tell my teens, "Only share online what you're comfortable shouting in a crowded movie theater."

When my daughter applied for a job with a marketing firm recently, they handed her a release form for access to her social media accounts. I asked her if this was common. She shared, "Absolutely. My girlfriend went in for her interview, and they asked her to sign on to her Facebook account so they could see it right then and there."

Is it legal? Can employers ask to see your teen's personal account? You bet your booty they can. The same way they can ask your teen to take a drug test or anything else required to land the position. Sure, your teen has the power to say no and refuse, but she stands the risk of losing the job to someone else. Make sure you convey to your teen that even the wittiest quip on Facebook has the power to follow her around for good or bad.

Think About It with Your Teen

Purpose. What's the purpose of being on a social network? Good reasons like hanging out online with friends or sharing photos with the grandparents can quickly become watching the lives of people they will probably never meet and who have little or no interest in them. Train them to limit their time online, and don't be afraid to give a social app a time-out if it's taking too much time away from real family relationships.

Precaution. Self-reflect before you self-reveal. I'm not sure we can impress this enough. When they shoot from the hip with pithy comments, they may think they're being funny, but oftentimes funny is lost in translation. I tell my teens, "Only share online what you're comfortable shouting in a crowded movie theater." The same can be said about texting.

Pretend. Remind your teen not everything they see is real. Truth isn't always found on the Internet. I remember someone telling me, "I was on your website. Your family takes such great pictures!" I chuckled and told her, "That's because I only put up the good ones." Our social interaction online doesn't always reflect real life. It's life happening the way people want you to perceive it.

Play It Safe

For those of you still wondering how to instill protective, practical social media boundaries for your teen, I thought we'd begin by tackling their Facebook page. I've made a list of things you should know and do.

Begin with honesty. In order to have a Facebook account, you must be thirteen years old and have a valid email address. Like I shared earlier, 7.5 million kids *under* thirteen in the United States are on Facebook.[1] Which means one of two things: either the children created a Facebook account without their parents' knowledge, or parents are okay with lying about their child's age. Parents, your kids are watching. This is your chance to lead by example. I can't expect my teenager to be honest online if I'm not.

Communicate. Before your teen opens a social network account, there needs to be some communication. This means sitting down and sharing the good, the bad, and the ugly about being online.

You can download a free social media contract from my website JoanneKraft.com. Discuss it and sign together. It's a great tool for opening up dialogue. Use it to guide you to create ground rules for social networking and to get some good communication going.

Use privacy settings. Review all of the options on the privacy settings page. Each social network has one. This is where you can choose who can see and interact with the information they share. You can be as selective as you want to be. If you're on Facebook, I'd recommend at the very least using the "Friends Only" option. That way your teen and you can control who they "Friend."

Preapprove tags. Here's another Facebook term. A tag is when a "Friend" puts up a photo or posts something on their page and can include your teen in it. Which means it would show up on their Facebook page for all their "Friends" to see. Preapproving tags allows your child to control just what photos or other information are being linked to their page.

Use notification settings. This is a great Facebook feature. You can set it up so you're notified of any activity performed using your child's name, including photo tags. In my opinion, you can never be too restrictive with your Facebook page.

Don't use push notifications. Facebook notifications are not the same as push notifications from other social media sources. When you download an app, it asks if you want push notifications. These are reminders in sound or text form that can be very distracting and quite rude if you're out in public.

Flying solo a no-go. Please don't allow your teen to fly solo on the Internet. Where Facebook is concerned, it won't be long before your teen begins collecting friends. My nineteen-year-old has 776 Facebook "friends," and he only knows a few dozen of them personally. The term "friend" is used quite loosely on Facebook. A computer in his bedroom is a bad idea. You wouldn't shut the door and leave your son with 776 friends alone, would you? Keep the social networking on the computer in the family common area. I have a law enforcement background—I should know.

My kids and I are connected on any social network they're on. This is nonnegotiable. I'm able to see what is happening in their life from time to time. What surprises me is just how much they share. When my oldest two were still in high school and living at home, they were like prison guards with their privacy. Shouting at anyone who didn't knock first, angry over an overheard conversation on the phone, and annoyed if we didn't respect their space. I think my husband summed it up perfectly: "I've never seen a generation so upset about losing their privacy, while voluntarily giving it away."

As a mom of teenagers, I don't want to be the *uncool,* old-fashioned mom. But I, too, was a teenager way back in the dark ages. The Internet can be a magical place, but it's also the spot where the young and naïve are taken advantage of. Country singer Brad Paisley has a great video from his song *Online* that sums up what a parent wants to convey in a humorous way. When he croons, "I'm so much cooler online," I nod along in agreement. I recommend watching it before you discuss signing a social media contract with your teenager. What a great icebreaker before sharing a few loving boundaries.

Worthy Conduct

I've said it before and I'll say it again—pay attention. What may seem like harmless time with friends could affect the joy your children once had. A study published by the journal *Cyberpsychology, Behavior, and Social Networking* found that people who spent less time socializing with friends in cyberspace and more time socializing with them in real life were less likely to report they were unhappy.[2] You know your teen better than anyone—just be aware.

As Christian parents, what words of godly wisdom can we encourage our kids with when it comes to social media? In Philippians, I believe I found my answer:

> Only let your conduct be worthy of the gospel of Christ, so that whether I come and see you or am absent, I may hear of your affairs, that you stand fast in one spirit, with one mind striving together for the faith of the gospel. (Phil. 1:27 NKJV)

Teenagers need their space. They need to be trusted. As a mean mom, I need to balance healthy interaction with them and fight the urge to be the Instagram-Twitter-Facebook police. I love this verse because the apostle Paul exhorts his friends to remember who they are in Christ. He doesn't threaten them with the consequences of an all-consuming God. He strengthens their hearts. That's what we need to do. Let's refresh our teenagers' memories. They are children of the Most High God. No matter where their feet tread or what their fingers type, they represent him.

Mom to Mom

How do you set loving boundaries for social media?

My middle-schooler wants to be on Facebook, but according to their policy you need to be thirteen and she's eleven. So, we're playing by the rules and saying no until thirteen, and then we'll reconsider. She's told me many times, "You are the meanest mom ever!" To which

I respond, "Good, you'll have something to talk to your therapist about." —KAREN DALY COOK, MFCC

℘ Rule number one for our teens: I set the password. I have access to their Facebook accounts, their cell phones, and any electronic device they come into contact with. My biggest concern? What others are sending them—are their conversations and photos God-honoring, honest, gossip-free? Is anyone bullying or trying to tempt them to sinful behavior? So far, their friends are amazing, kind, good kids, which is a powerful reassurance for this over-protective mommy. —ELIZABETH THOMPSON

℘ In some aspects, parenting is more challenging because we battle the technology beast. It fights for time away from quality time to build relationships and adds to parental worries, I believe. Yes, we can control it to some degree, but only so far. —RACHAEL MCKINNEY

Notes

[1] "Generation M2: Media in the Lives of 8- to 18-Year-Olds," Henry J. Kaiser Family Foundation, January 20, 2010, http://kff.org/other/event /generation-m2-media-in-the-lives-of.

[2] Mary Ann Liebert, *Cyberpsychology, Behavior, and Social Networking: The Impact of the Internet, Multimedia and Virtual Reality on Behavior and Society* (New Rochelle, NY: Mary Ann Liebert, 1998).

CHAPTER TWENTY

Mean Moms Focus on the Future

When you are the recipient of the moniker, meanest mom, or something similar, then you know you are probably doing a great job parenting.

—**Barbara Rainey**

Jane Hambleton has dubbed herself *the meanest mom on the planet*. After finding alcohol in her son's car, she decided to sell the car and placed an ad in the local newspaper.

OLDS 1999 Intrigue.
Totally uncool parents who obviously don't love teenage son, selling his car. Only driven for three weeks before snoopy mom who needs to get a life found booze under front seat. $3,700/offer. Call meanest mom on the planet.[1]

After the ad was published, Jane fielded over seventy phone calls from emergency room technicians, school counselors, and a bevy of parents congratulating her for being so responsible. Not one caller claimed she was too strict.

Mean moms are all around us. Only a few make the news. Most of us live behind the scenes. Marci Seither is one of them.

"I was having a serious parenting issue . . . with my son's underwear. I couldn't stand the sight of Scott's multi-stripe boxers billowing out of the top of his low-slung jeans. I would have told him to put a belt on, but he already had one on. To be totally honest, I think it was weighted to help him reach full sagging potential."

"Hey," I said one day. "Your underwear is showing."

"So?" he replied, as if he was stunned I hadn't gotten the memo that sagging drawers was now *cool*.

"So don't do it. It's a lack of self-respect," I replied. "That's why it is called under wear. It's meant to be worn *under* what you wear."

He gave me a primal grunt before adding, "Everyone wears their pants like this." He went on to say, "Mom, I think the only person who has an issue with it is you. It's not a big deal."

The next morning, Scott came rushing out of the bathroom after brushing his teeth. He knocked on my bedroom door to let me know it was time for me to drive him and his younger sister to school.

"I'm getting dressed," I responded. "Out in a minute." I opened my bedroom door and walked down the hall to get my car keys and purse.

My son popped his head out of his bedroom. His eyes widened with sheer terror. I'm sure he never imagined what my fuchsia-colored bra would look like on the *outside* of a yellow T-shirt. But, now he did.

"What are you doing?" he finally spoke up.

"I'm taking you to school," I smiled.

"Not dressed like that," he stammered.

"Everyone wears things like this," I said. "It's not a big deal."

I put on my sunglasses and headed for the door. "Son, I think you're the only one who has an issue with it."

He reached back and pulled his pants up.

What sets a mean mom apart from the pack? Shock-and-awe parenting. That's what we call it in our home. Every once in a while, you need to shock your kids and follow through with what you said you'd do. Kids need to think, *My mom just might be crazy enough to do this.*

Jane Hambleton gave her son two rules when he bought his car: no alcohol and keep it locked. He didn't keep his part of the deal. Her response shocked her son and became awe-inspiring to the rest of us. My guess is, the next time her son will believe her when she lays down a few loving boundaries.

Don't Be Surprised When Hell Breaks Loose

There is no greater ministry than raising a child. May I share a little cautionary wisdom? When God is on the move and the ministry of motherhood is on your heart, all hell will break loose. Count on it.

No matter where I sign up to serve or what I decide to do, the moment I dig in and attempt to fulfill that *something*, it's a guarantee our car will break down, one of the kids will get a cold, or Paul and I will argue about something ridiculously silly. I've come to expect it. Motherhood is no different.

Recently, I spoke at a women's conference in the Smoky Mountains. A four-hour drive from our house, the location was breathtaking. The women were incredibly

What sets a mean mom apart from the pack? Shock-and-awe parenting. That's what we call it in our home. Every once in a while, you need to shock your kids and follow through with what you said you'd do. Kids need to think, My mom just might be crazy enough to do this.

kind, and everything seemed to be going perfectly *until day two*. A telephone call home exposed a family emergency, and though I knew my husband could handle it, I was sick to my stomach with worry.

Sometimes offering yourself as a vessel for the presence and work of God is costly. —JOHN ORTBERG

My heart began to pound and thoughts tormented me. *What an awful mother you are. How can you face these ladies and speak when all hell is breaking loose at home?*

I made my way back to my room and the Lord got an earful. *Why would you bring me four hours away from my family when they need me?* I had no desire to leave my room or face the women. After many tears, the Lord's answer to my frantic prayers and fretful thoughts came through his Word.

> It was just before the Passover Festival. Jesus knew that the hour had come for him to leave this world and go to the Father. Having loved his own who were in the world, he loved them to the end.
>
> The evening meal was in progress, and the devil had already prompted Judas, the son of Simon Iscariot, to betray Jesus. Jesus knew that the Father had put all things under his power, and that he had come from God and was returning to God; so he got up from the meal, took off his outer clothing, and wrapped a towel around his waist. After that, he poured water into a basin and began to wash his disciples' feet, drying them with the towel that was wrapped around him. (John 13:1–5)

The devotion attached to this verse continued God's silent encouragement to persevere:

> Adversity invites leaders to lead. It is your time to trust the Lord and lead by faith, not fear. In hard times a leader asks, "Will I panic or pray?" "Will I stay calm or be sucked into the chaos?" "Will I serve the team or stay secluded in silence?" Jesus faced death, but He was determined to stay focused on His heavenly Father and the mission at hand. Adversity is an opportunity to prove the point of Providence. Christ is in control.[2]

Jesus knew Judas had left to return with soldiers. He was fully aware of the few hours before he would experience a horrific crucifixion and *all hell would break loose.*

Still, he calmly served.

A mother is a ministry leader. Is there anything more frightening to the enemy of our souls than a woman who raises her children to stand up for God and against this eternal foe? So why are you surprised at the fiery ordeal that has come on you to test you, as though something strange were happening to you? (1 Pet. 4:12).

Remember, all hell breaks loose when God's greatest work is at hand. Consider trials in your motherhood ministry a backhanded compliment of the enemy. Do not crumble in defeat. You are a worthy enough adversary to oppose or you wouldn't be attacked. Do not panic or get sucked into the chaos.

The world responded to Christ's greatest ministry work on the cross with complete darkness and earthquakes. So why are we surprised to encounter trials in our ministry of mothering? Be encouraged with an earthquake or two. It's a holy response to God's work and your service.

The world responded to Christ's greatest ministry work on the cross with complete darkness and earthquakes. So why are we surprised to encounter trials in our ministry of mothering? Be encouraged with an earthquake or two. It's a holy response to God's work and your service.

Pray and persevere. God can give you all you need to overcome any obstacle. There is a cost to ministry. Christ is our example. But, like our Savior, we must continue to feed and serve the sheep (our children) and consider it an honor when we come up against unholy opposition.

As for me and the women's conference? I thanked God for the trial that almost derailed my weekend. I praised him for his Word and newfound peace. I washed my face and put on a little lipstick, then finished another day. Those dear women never knew the struggle I faced. With all hell breaking loose, I washed the feet of his sheep.

Temporary discomfort is just that, temporary. There's a greater goal in sight, to bring up a child to be independent, hardworking, and responsible—and faith is the ribbon weaving together all the pieces. In humility, God receives the glory in the end. Her children watch her faith play out in living color.

Mean Moms See the Future

What sets a mean mom apart? Her eyes are on the future.

I asked a few mean moms what kind of legacy they want to leave their kids. What did they think was important for their children to know? Here are a few of their answers:

> Lately, I feel like my legacy is being on the computer all of the time, and then getting on their case the rest of it. I hate that. I had all these grand visions of

motherhood but am finding that my expectations of who I was supposed to be keep getting in the way of who I turned out to be. I want to be remembered as fun, loving, and a mom who relied on her faith during those trials and hardships—a mom who sought prayer and trusted God for everything. —JENNY SULPIZIO

That my love for them was endless and unconditional and God's love is even more. —KATIE CHANEY

God believes in you. —MICHELLE BUSCHINI

I love you. Dad loves you. God loves you more. Jesus died for you. The end. —ADELLE GABRIELSON

To know how much they are loved by God that he gave his Son. How much I love them. I hope they remember me as the president of their fan club and biggest cheerleader. —MITZI LIMBURG

#1. God loves you and accepts you, and created you just the way you are.

#2. To always strive to do your best and to serve God and others.

#3. To use the gifts he has given you for his glory. I want to be remembered as a mom who loved my child very much, and tried to teach her good values, and I want her to remember the fun times. I want her to see the world as an adventure, and to embrace the diversity and deliciousness all around her. —DEANN OKAMURA

I want my kids to know two things:

1. God loves them and is always there for them, even if their circumstances suggest otherwise.

2. I love them more than words, and nothing will ever change that. —LINDSEY BELL

I would tell them the same thing my mother told me: "People may fail and disappoint you. Keep your eyes on Jesus. He will never fail or disappoint you." Hebrews 12:1–3: "Therefore, since we are surrounded by such a great cloud of witnesses, let us throw off everything that hinders and the sin that so easily entangles. And let us run with perseverance the race marked out for us, fixing our eyes on Jesus, the pioneer and perfecter of faith. For the joy set before him he endured the cross, scorning its shame, and sat down at the right hand of the throne of God. Consider him who endured such opposition from sinners, so that you will not grow weary and lose heart."
—SAUNDRIA KECK

My legacy as their mom? I'll die making sure they know the way home. —ELAINE OLSEN

I want my kids to live life for an audience of One. My twelve-year-old daughter told me her friend said, "I think your family are real Christians." This girl sees others who claim to be Christians, but notices they don't live out what they say they believe. On days that I think I'm struggling as a mom, I will remember this: When we live for God and not someone else, it shows—and others notice. —ANN GOADE

The number one thing I want my daughter to know is Matthew 7:13–14 because of Matthew 16:24–27.
—JESSICA KING

I want my kids to remember they had a mom who loved their daddy, loved God, and even when I went through tough times I never gave up. —KRISTINE RASOR

℮I used to worry about teaching my children how to behave in public, how to act/eat/dress, etc., in a way that honored the family and didn't bring embarrassment. Now, I realize, much of that is caught, not taught. The goal should not be to bring honor to the family but to bring honor to God. I want my children to remember me as someone who loved the Lord—someone who shone with the Light of the Lord. I hope to be remembered as a loving mom full of grace and mercy yet strong enough to discipline out of love. —SARA MUNDAY

℮I want my daughter to know she will always be safe and loved by God. When I think about my legacy I get emotional and weepy, because I can't think about the legacy I want to leave my daughter without thinking about the legacy my mom shows me. I want to be remembered as my mother's daughter, who is just like her; strong, creative, loving, kind, generous, and faithful. —KRISTINE MOUL

℮My legacy is that my two children know they're loved by their Heavenly Father and by me. And, they remember me as being a great mom who followed the Lord no matter what happened. I want them to remember how much fun we had together and this includes all the crazy southern sayings (that I learned from my parents). Most especially? That I taught them to love. —CATHY SIMPKINS

℮Jesus is their Lord and to remember he loves them— the small stuff doesn't matter. I want their faith to be the most important thing and to always stand up for what they believe in. I want to be remembered as a mom of faith who was patient. —LAURIE HAYS

⁀That I love them and believe in them and my love and belief in them represents God's love and belief in them— neither are reversible or because of what they have or haven't done. I want them to know how much they're worth and to never sell themselves short of that worth. I hope they remember me loving God and loving people.

—ASHLEY GERHARD

What about you? What will your parenting legacy be? The ministry of motherhood is holy ground. God gave this child to you. He chose you. He handpicked you for this job.

Do you feel beaten and battle worn? Are you tired? Then you're probably doing something right. Mom, this is the most exhausting and excruciating ministry work there is and the most rewarding. If you feel like quitting—don't. Each day brings new mercy (Lam. 3:22–23). You were selected to guide and grow this small person into adulthood, which means God believes you can do this.

And, from what I hear, there's been whispers of great rewards for our faithful duty and hard mothering work, payment even more incredibly amazing than our hearts can hold—*grandchildren*.

This is not the time to be a gooey-sweet marshmallow or to back away from parenting when it's hard. Be strong. Be courageous. Never fear being called *mean* by your son or daughter. Stand firm, dig in, do not waver, and always remember—mean moms raise great kids.

Notes

1 Associated Press, "'Meanest Mom' Sells Car after Finding Liquor," nbcnews. com, last updated January 9, 2008, www.nbcnews.com/id/22578679/ns/us_news-life/t/meanest-mom-sells-car-after-finding-liquor/#.U0yd-5VOXmI.

2 This quote is from an email daily devotional sent by Wisdom Hunters in 2013.

Joanne Kraft believes in strengthening women through the love of Christ. She'd love the opportunity to share at your next women's ministry event, community group, or MOPS gathering.

Contact her at JoanneKraft@gmail.com.

Don't forget to sign up for Joanne's monthly email newsletter and receive a FREE Mean Mom Bill of Rights and Mean Mom Social Media Contract at JoanneKraft.com.

Blessed is she who has believed that the Lord would fulfill his promises to her. —LUKE 1:45

Below are wonderful resources to help navigate your mothering journey. Make sure to check them out.

FamilyLife.com

TheMomInitiative.com

FocusontheFamily.com

SpirituallyUnequalMarriage.com

MomLifeToday.com

MotheringfromScratch.com

HeartsatHome.org

GraceforMoms.com

Proverbs31.org

MOPS.org

"*This* is the book that I so desperately needed as a young mom. Joanne gives moms permission and encouragement to do what they know in their hearts they need to do—set boundaries and stand firm when the going gets tough. Joanne writes from hard-won wisdom, compassion, and with a refreshing and disarming sense of humor. It will change your mothering."

—**Melinda Means,** co-author of *Mothering From Scratch*

"Joanne's laugh-out-loud humor and transparency filled my mama's heart with joy and hope. A 'mean mom' is a mother who will raise her children to become young men and women who step into adulthood with honor, respect, love, and godly character. A must read for every mom."

—**Lynn Donovan,** author of *Winning Him Without Words* and *Not Alone*

"Joanne proves that mean truly is the new black . . . it looks good on everyone and comes in your size. Her new book politely introduces old-school parenting tools to modern-day mama hearts."

—**Teasi Cannon,** author of *My Big Bottom Blessing*

"I highly recommend this book for any mom who knows that God has big plans for her kids and will do whatever it takes to make sure those plans come to fruition."

—**Erin MacPherson,** author of *Hot Mama* and The Christian Mama's Guide series

"The mean mom may not be liked by her children for the day, but she will be loved and respected for a lifetime."

—**Kathy Helgemo,** author of *Mothering from Scratch*

"For young moms, this book is like sitting for hours with a trusted mentor. For experienced moms, this book is a field manual for walking out the toughest days on the job. A must-read for all mothers—especially softies like me."

—**Jessica Wolstenholm,** co-author, *The Pregnancy Companion* and *The Baby Companion* and co-founder, graceformoms.com

"Joanne's engaging and humorous writing is packed with practical wisdom for women who want to be 'mean,' successful moms. She shows us how to parent with our children's future in mind."

—**Kathy Howard,** author of 6 books, including *God Is My Refuge*

"With her relatable voice, words of encouragement, and sparkling wit, the adventure known as motherhood just got a whole lot easier . . ."

—**Jenny Lee Sulpizio,** author of *For the Love of God* and *Confessions of a Wonder Woman Wannabe*